FIELD GUIDE: HOW TO BE A
GRAPHIC DESIGNER

ROCKPORT

Copyright © 2009 by maomao publications
First published in 2008 in the United States of America by
Rockport Publishers, a member of
Quayside Publishing Group
100 Cummings Center
Suite 406-L
Beverly, MA 01915-6101
Telephone: (978) 282-9590
Fax: (978) 283-2742
www.rockpub.com

ISBN-13: 978-1-59253-490-6
ISBN-10: 1-59253-490-2

10 9 8 7 6 5 4 3 2 1

Publisher: Paco Asensio
Editorial coordination: Anja Llorella Oriol
Authors: Ana Labudovic, Nenad Vukusic
Proofreader: Cindy Blazevic
Illustration: José Manuel Hortelano Pi
Art director: Emma Termes Parera
Layout: Gemma Gabarron Vicente
English translation: Heather Bagott

Editorial project:
maomao publications
Tallers, 22 bis, 3º 1ª
08001 Barcelona, Spain
Tel.: +34 93 481 57 22
Fax: +34 93 317 42 08
www.maomaopublications.com

Printed in Singapore

FIELD GUIDE: HOW TO BE A
GRAPHIC DESIGNER

BEVERLY MASSACHUSETTS

ROCKPORT PUBLISHERS

Contents

YOU ARE A...

Studio owner = 9.0%

Freelance = 20.2%

Employed in a studio-agency = 49.9%

Student = 17.8%

Intern = 3.1%

INTRODUCTION

Universal rules apply in any book that tries to tell you how to be better at what you do. Doing well on a job interview or landing more clients involve the same basic how-to's for a lawyer, milkman, or a designer.

We are not here to serve you a piping hot success recipe.

Even though most of what we say in these pages is common sense and to some extent applicable to other professions, it focuses on the area of graphic design and its intricacies. It has no definitive answers and offers no linear path to success, but rather shares the experiences of the authors and of all the great people who helped us put together this guide.

We've cross-examined our interviewees to see how they cope with the stress, get along with their colleagues, handle clients, break free, boost their creativity, and much, much more. All of the interviews are complimented with the work that best represents their studio/self. After all, you're the visual type that prefers seeing what lies behind the words.

Are you a student, freelancer, employed, or someone else? Which field have you specialized in? Are you happy with what you do? These and about twenty other questions comprised a survey conducted on professional designers and students, helping us create a picture of the present situation in the profession.

In all, 2,096 participants from around the world provided us with information on their work habits, likes and dislikes—all to your advantage. You won't find surgically precise statistics about their salaries or employment rates, but rather their opinions about everyday dilemmas and long-term plans. And guess what they all had in common? A desire to enjoy their work and to be able to live from it.

Being a virtuoso on your computer and eating grids for breakfast just won't do anymore, so, if you are sure you have what it takes to be a great graphic designer, we are here to prepare you for the journey and help you to take those first few steps. Remember us when you become rich and famous, because we were the ones who broke our backs trying to tell you how to break yours!

HOW MANY HOURS A WEEK DO YOU WORK?

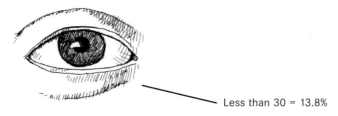

Less than 30 = 13.8%

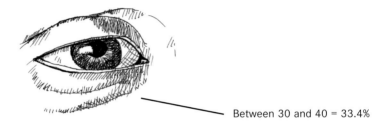

Between 30 and 40 = 33.4%

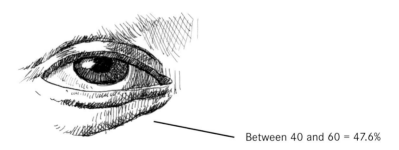

Between 40 and 60 = 47.6%

More?? = 5.2%

WAS GRAPHIC DESIGN YOUR FIRST CAREER CHOICE?

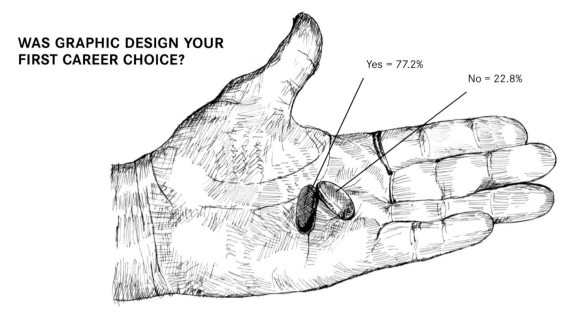

Yes = 77.2%

No = 22.8%

AT WHAT AGE DID YOU START WORKING?

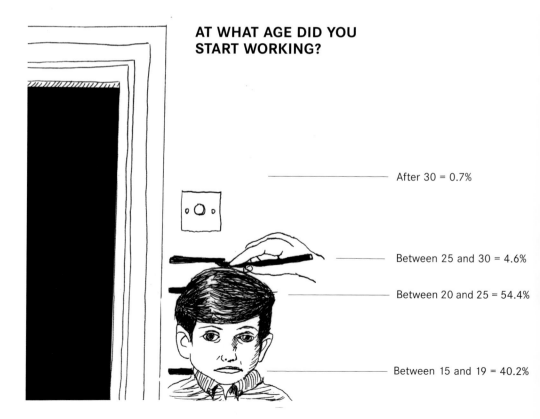

After 30 = 0.7%

Between 25 and 30 = 4.6%

Between 20 and 25 = 54.4%

Between 15 and 19 = 40.2%

GRAPHIC DESIGN(ERS)

Everything is being designed, everyone can be a designer, design is ubiquitous, everywhere, overrated and underrated. Design is the future, clients not only want your "graphic designing," but also your "design thinking" to solve problems that have nothing to do with design. Designers are... more pressured than ever?

It's kind of tricky to find your voice when there is so much tangential thinking. Plus there's very little mystery left in what a designer does and how he does it given all the plethora of available technology. Yet, for the very same reason there is an ever greater need for great designers, for professionals who are strong in more than one thing, and for people who are capable of thinking outside the box, around the box, and without the box, to find new solutions to old problems, communication or otherwise.

There are so many fields to cover, and so little time. Will you try finding your niche or will you try evolving your multidisciplinary skills?

Wherever you are in your professional career, however old or experienced you might be, the truth is that you will have to work hard, gain weight, and lose sleep. And you will create your own definition of success along the way.

Omnipresent in the Present

The amount of visual input we receive daily is growing exponentially. New advertising surfaces, products and media channels are becoming increasingly available, as graphic design infiltrates everything everywhere, expanding into a plethora of nooks and crannies of everyday life. More than ever, there is a need for someone to design these means of visual communication, to render them more visible, usable, and powerful.

"Advertising is everywhere. Books are commonplace. Billions of people use the Web every day. I believe there is an innate desire in people to create. And the most logical things to create are those with which people surround themselves," says Frank Chimero.

According to the U.S. Bureau of Labor Statistics, the employment of graphic designers is expected to grow 10 percent from 2006 to 2016, as demand for graphic design increases from advertisers, publishers, and computer design firms. This is equal to the rate of average growth for all occupations.[1]

The appeal of graphic design as a profession is not surprising. From the outside it appears easy: you sit in front of a computer, work some magic, and with a little bit of help from your programs – voilà! – there it is, your creation. And you get paid for it. Once you actually start practicing conjuring this art of imagery, however, the sheen wears off. The light bulb doesn't flash above your head instantly every time you sit down to solve a design problem, your clients do not always understand your ideas, the projects you adore do not really pay the bills. And all you ever wanted was to have some fun working on interesting projects for good clients. Was that too much to ask?

The day you decided to dedicate your professional—and probably a big chunk of your personal—life to graphic design you signed up for a test of endurance. Numerous sleepless nights, a steady stream of junk food, a few ruined relationships, 15 minutes of fame, and a bad back are frequently an essential part of the package.

But it's not all bad. The passion that drives the act of creation is a source of enthusiasm, and enthusiasm is the spark and the fire that burns away all the aches and pains. For, being a graphic designer is not only a job; many would say it's a calling.

As it consumes a major part of your life, it will become personal. Yet, the forbidden fruit of mixing business and pleasure sometimes yields special and rewarding projects. The ardent rela-

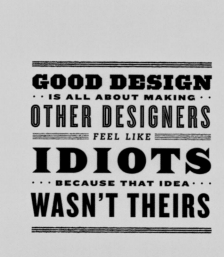

GOOD DESIGN
· · IS ALL ABOUT MAKING · ·
OTHER DESIGNERS
FEEL LIKE
IDIOTS
· · · BECAUSE THAT IDEA · · ·
WASN'T THEIRS

REMEMBER!
LOOKING IS NOT
AT DESIGN IS
MAKING
DESIGN

My profession allows me to be as creative as possible.

Tiny text down here™

PEOPLE IGNORE DESIGN
THAT IGNORES PEOPLE.

Frank Chimero: Inspirational Design Posters (self-initiated, 2008)

Frank Chimero
Designer and illustrator
Missouri
Inspired by the mid-century aesthetic, Frank tries to recapture the sense of optimism, playfulness, heart, and charm. He can usually be found surrounded by many tiny slips of paper with fragments of ideas scrawled on them. He thinks playing and noticing are crucial parts of the creative process, and he tries to remind himself that he gets paid to play and notice things.
www.makemakemake.org

tionship designers have with their work sometimes gives them almost bipolar traits; one minute they are arrogant and self-righteous about their projects and methods, they brag about their clients to other clients and colleagues, criticize and undermine the work of other designers, but as soon as they feel jeopardized by their competition they become incredibly insecure.

They refuse to show how much they care about their colleagues' opinions, complain about unqualified newbies stealing their work, and avoid sharing their experiences because they fear divulging the secrets of the trade.

Frank Chimero explains it in the following fashion:

"I think arrogance is usually a by-product of insecurity. But what do you expect? For designers to do good work, they have to pour themselves into it, and there is always the possibility of rejection. It's easy to make the correlation that the rejection of your work is also a small rejection of you as a person. It's your idea, after all. It's a tightrope walk, and I think that even professional tightrope walkers are scared of falling every now and then. I know I'm disappointed, sad, and sometimes angry when my hard work gets shot down with just a word.

"I think the traits of arrogance and insecurity are not necessarily specific to designers. I think you'd be just as likely to meet a lawyer or an accountant with those characteristics. The difference is that designers are spoonfed the idea that they have this grand impact on culture and, ultimately, the world. The arrogance may come from

that. After all, changing the world is serious business. The insecurity may stem from the fact that we'll never live up to those lofty (and possibly unreasonable) expectations.

"I've let go of the belief that my work has a grand impact on culture and the idea that I have to change the world. I think my work has gotten better because of it. Now, I just try to make myself and my audience happy by being honest with them and with myself."

You need the opinions of your colleagues and clients, and you need to pay attention to your audience in order to get perspective and develop, but if you take everything too seriously and worry too much about what others think you might have a rough time doing your job well and enjoying it.

The people from Digital Kitchen took some time and effort to make the hilarious campaign Designer//Slash // Model, which tackles the subject of glorifying the design profession. Jeff Long, the executive creative director at Digital Kitchen Chicago explained:

"It began as an open-ended assignment to create a Digital Kitchen company video for Stash. There was a

Digital Kitchen: Designer//Slash//Model (self-initiated, 2007)

Digital Kitchen
Creative agency
New York/Chicago/Seattle/Los Angeles
Digital Kitchen is a creative agency that focuses on film production, experiential design, motion graphics, brand identity, and interactive work for marketing and entertainment. They stretch from strategy and messaging to concept development and execution in just about any medium—including skywriting, which we view as underutilized and often poorly designed.
www.d-kitchen.com

Digital Kitchen: The Company Main Title
(TNT/ScottFree/John Calley Productions, 2008)

Digital Kitchen: 12th Annual Webby Awards
(live show content, 2008)

short turnaround so we immediately focused on two ideas: do another montage of our most recent work or a short film about Digital Kitchen.

"We decided to do the short film but feared the awful art-speak that turns every creative agency, musician, or actor who talks about 'their process' or 'the work' into pretentious dweebs. We created Designer//Slash//Model to poke fun at the business—and to save us from ourselves.

"The reaction was immediate, voluminous, and overwhelmingly positive. There were quite a few people who took it seriously but they were usually 'outed' in the blogs for their lack of comedic sophistication.

"We like multi-talented problem solvers— conceptual people who want to grow and learn new ways of communicating ideas.

"We're not looking for Designer// Slash//Models."

Graphic Design Today

The birth of desktop publishing in the mid-1980s changed the face of design forever. Suddenly, designers had access to a faster and cheaper way to create and manipulate graphic material without the need for many resources (material and human) or expensive and complex techniques (such as hand-rendering or paste-ups on paper type-setters). Lengthy and sometimes painful apprenticeships were no longer mandatory to be able to work as a designer. Computers embraced a number of traditional techniques, offering instant results and overall efficiency. Production costs dropped, production turnover grew, and computers became a designer's best friend, revolutionizing the industry in the process.

The rigidity of rules in the professional world of graphic design relaxed now that everyone had a computer and Adobe Photoshop installed on it. Richard Niessen from Niessen & de Vries studio complains that unprofessional clients think designers can design a book in a day, and make corrections in a minute, while they wait, on a Sunday afternoon.

"There are no more technical walls behind which we can hide... Since the clients have color screens and color printers most think in full color. They forget the fact that print work is about reproduction, and that you can play with it. On the other hand: they recognize that what we do is far more creative than whatever they can do in their free time."

The magic is gone. Clients can now ask their little nephews to come up with a quick solution based on their ideas and desires. It makes you exposed to unjustified scrutiny, creates a certain tension in your relations with clients, especially when you're young and inexperienced and you don't really know how (or dare) to confront them.

Richard Niessen: New Year card (Stedelijk Museum Amsterdam, 2007)

Niessen & de Vries
Studio
Amsterdam, The Netherlands
Esther de Vries and Richard Niessen share an interest in intense collaborations with clients. Shying from mere representation, they tend to produce "new" works, and make extensive use of the printing process. Instead of one clear concept they seek durability through richness in layers, emphasize the materiality of the print work and avoid references.
www.niessendevries.nl

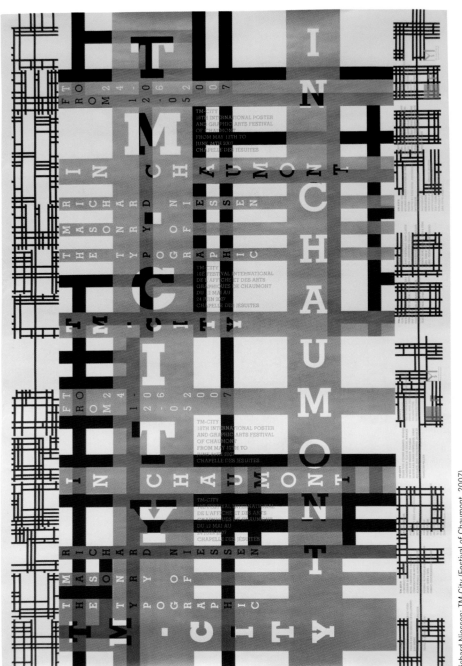

Richard Niessen: TM-City (Festival of Chaumont, 2007)

Peer Pressure

Looking at the portfolios of your design heroes or reading their interviews, it is difficult not to fall under the impression that they glide elegantly from one cool project to another, completing each and every one with perfection and ease, that their clients love whatever comes out of their studios, and that they have time to work on personal projects.

As soon as you scratch beneath the surface you realize how little of it is true—all designers face the same issues and passed through the same initiation of blood, sweat, and tears before becoming successful. This process is not measured by money or clients, but by growth and progression, which comes after doing your best.

Excellent designers will always get good work and good clients. Nowadays achieving that excellence means doing more than sweating in front of the screen. Where to begin? How to profile yourself? What happens if creative juices dry up? How to make sure you can pay the bills at the end of the month? What if the client doesn't like the end product?

Relax, you can do it. Your position isn't any better or worse than that of anyone else. It's about your attitude and flexibility. You might have all the right degrees from all the right schools, twenty years of experience and six studios behind you—but you'll still be learning the rules as long as you're in the game.

Be brave and curious, push yourself harder, find new ways to improve your work, and don't be scared to explore. Being open to opportunities means taking risks. You're bound to fall flat on your face a few times, but you'll learn more from that experience than from sitting still. And that is still less painful than missing out on an opportunity.

Remember that it takes a long time to create something worthwhile, and investing in yourself is the best thing you can do.

Versatility vs. Specialization

The search for original ideas and visual solutions will never end. As modern technologies blur the boundaries between various media, myriad styles and techniques become available.

In order to do your job as a freelancer or as a part of a team you need to harness the skills of a project manager, accountant, copywriter, seller, architect, psychologist, as well as a typesetter, photographer, illustrator, color expert, and filmmaker. Not only do you need to be familiar with the history of graphic design, but also with the world around you. (Let's be honest, many of you are blessed with the curiosity to explore new cultures, areas, and mediums, so this is hardly a burden. In fact, it can only reflect positively on what you do.)

Graphic design isn't about doing one job. It's about doing a dozen of them. The more you know, encounter, utilize, and apply, the more you are worth. If it is a spice of life, it can sure spice up the design. The same way that knowing a foreign language helps you learn new ones and each new one gets easier to master, switching between various fields of graphic design as well as embracing the ones surrounding it (such as project management or pub

lic relations) gives you self-confidence and gets you prepared to tackle new problems.

Yet, it hardly seems possible to train in all those areas and start working before turning fifty. And by trying to grasp so many walks of life, is your quality of work being jeopardized? Does being a successful graphic designer mean that at some point you will have to choose between becoming a jack of all trades (and master of none) and a specialist?

Yes and no. Yes, it is possible—and, no... not in all those areas. You will always remain an amateur in some of the fields you try, but considering the word "amateur" translates from the French "lover of"—that is, one who performs for pleasure rather than money—you will explore those areas not for money but out of curiosity and love of new experiences. And in your line of work new experiences are a blessing. Even if you choose to specialize at some point, your forays of amateurism in other fields can serve as an inspiration or a guideline for future projects.

When you secure your first client the last thing you want to think about is copywriting and accounting. You'll want to explore the topography of graphic design and find your niche.

It's my second day at work so still I really don't know it

I LIKE what I'm doing, otherwise I WOULDN'T do it.

The money is good, sometimes the work is fun, sometimes it SUCKS

HAPPINES IS A WARM GUN

both OK but not from the ≡HEART≡

♥ Love it ♥ as long as I'm getting by, money isn't much of an issue

My boss is aging an loving grip on what works and what doesn't works

I ♥ my job and I earn just enough. I wish I earned more though

I am a student. I do not earn any money. I support myself by working in a cafe and a bar

IT'S COOL BUT CHAOTIC

love it hate it

IT'S ALL GOOD!!

I want better projects and more money

IT'S HARD AS HELL but i am masochist :)

I LIVE IT

the work is good but there's never enough time.

Feel like King of the Jungle

I don't like where I work and I don't like the place I work at. they lied about the position.

i worry that i'm not working quickly am well enough

Still a student but waiting for a promising future

As a student I do not get paid for my job, but it's a labour of LOVE!♡

IL PAYS LHE BILLS

I really shouldn't complain...

Heavenly Satisfied

I LOVE MY JOB!

I want more

i don't like my BOSS

I'm still a student and my current fast food job SUCKS!!

I like what I do, but my current position is in a bit of a hostile work enviroment.

I AM SO HAPPY WITH MY JOB!!

I love it even though I don't make enough money

I make good money, but I want more creative projects

the WORK I have is the worst design job on the face of planet. I work for republicans that pay me 8 USD a year

Well, it's not a real job yet, since I'm only fourteen. But I do make other peoples business cars and web sites, and it's something I love doing.

Everything's going ok, but a little less work and a little more money would be great

I LOVE WHAT I DO

In theory, the more terrain you cover, the greater the chance of new projects rolling in.

The Jack of All Trades

Versatility isn't necessarily something you choose consciously—it can also be a chain reaction. Let's say that a client approaches you in need of a logo for his company. He is pleased with the effort and the thought you have put into the look for his company, so he wants you to do his website as well as the annual report, but if possible make the binding special and design a new typeface specially for this occasion. Oh, and while you are at it, come up with some nice packaging for their new product line launch, too.

To do that well you need to do more than just apply the logo in various ways. You need to research the context and the medium, experiment, and teach yourself new tricks. If you do your homework well you will learn so much more about your client, his product or service, not to mention prep yourself for jobs. Be open to new knowledge and experiences.

You learn most by doing, taking on each project as a mini crash course in each subject you cover. As you learn, you gain confidence in your abilities.

Even though in some situations the process of learning, for example, how to write a style sheet for a website, might take away much of your time, you'll probably learn more under the pressure of a looming deadline than in a CSS workshop.

On the other hand, you might do a sloppy job and never really decide to learn how to do things better next time, turning you into a master of none. Persistence is important. You should never give up after a first failure. It is human to make mistakes, as much as it is human to get up and get on with it. Not even geniuses get it right the first time.

You must be able to decipher cultural signs and human behavior in order to create functional objects. Though it might seem like common sense, we cannot stress enough the importance of understanding and defining a problem clearly. Only after this has been accomplished can you move onto formatting the message and wielding your medium to its full extent. In simple words, know what are you trying to say, to whom and how, regardless of whether you are working on a poster or a signalization system. News reporters have five Ws and an H: who, what, where, when, why, and how. Designers should take those into consideration as well.

Giving physical form to ideas, as creators, you have to know exactly what the idea is. They come in various shapes and formats and can be expressed in an equal variety, depending on the target audience: passersby, subscribers, or clients. Choose the appropriate solutions for each and every one of them.

Being able to understand consumer trends, marketing, and manufacturing technologies makes you a corporate polyglot. Use this talent to build bridges between different professionals. This does not mean you have to wear your corporate hat forever, just that you are able to help solve problems. And, according to some definitions of graphic design, *that* is what you actually do—solve communication problems.

Taking photographs for editorials one day and coding action scripts the next can work as long as you do not freak out about the multitude of work that piles up, and are capable of multithreading. Learn to admit that you are not capable of doing everything solo and seek help if you feel a project is not progressing well, even after several tries. These situations happen all the time because designers tend to be control freaks. They want to be in charge of the entire process, do not trust other people with their tasks, and do not want to share the cake or the glory. But it doesn't have to be that way. Think about it, the worst thing to do would be to waste a lot of time only to learn that you cannot do it, losing the confidence of your clients in the process.

For instance, if you say you will take the photos for a clothing catalog as well as the design, and you botch up the job, you're in trouble. Then you're left alone (panicking) looking for someone to do another shoot for you, which would kill your budget, or spend days and days retouching the images into a half-decent look.

Or you can begin by planning things well, hiring a professional photographer, whose portfolio you would present to the client and whose fee you would include in your budget, which would allow you to concentrate on your part of the work and produce excellent material.

The moral of this story? Experimenting is good, but at some point you need to calculate the pros and cons and make educated guesses before your experiment blows up in your face and burns the lab to the ground.

The Specialist

Apart from having a better chance of securing more work, being capable of working across disciplines keeps you entertained, as jumping from one discipline to another is seldom boring.

On the other hand, we've learned from Adam Smith that specialized workers are more productive than people who try to do everything. A pioneering political economist, Smith was the founder of free-market economics. He believed labor was paramount, and that a division of labor would achieve a great increase in production. One example he used was the manufacturing of pins. One worker could probably make only 20 pins per day. However, if 10 people divided up the 18 steps required to make a pin they could make 48,000 pins in one day.[2] On the other hand, Smith also concluded that an excessive division of labor—that is, handling monotonous and repetitive tasks—would negatively affect a worker's intellect.

Back to our domain. Sure, a single person can do both the visuals and information architecture, but such efforts will rarely match the quality of work done by dedicated specialists.

But does that equate specialization with narrowing down your options? Can there ever be too much of a good thing? Everyone has to discover his or her own answer to this question. The greater variety of activities you do, the less time you'll devote to learning the intricacies of each—and the less experience you'll build with each one.

Focus is easier to find when you have found a field of specialty, and professional development becomes a clearer path on which to walk.

As *The Princeton Review* recommends in a description of its design curriculum: "Choosing a specialty is the name of the game, either in website design, product or packaging design, material use, or object arrangement."

Becoming an expert in a particular field means that at some point you will know or be able to build a dialogue or a network with other specialists in the field and share the wealth of expert knowledge between you.

You can choose your specialty based on a particular niche market without a saturated workforce—for example, becoming an exclusive specialist in the design of recyclable packaging for organic food. To use a more familiar field of expertise, you could design a CD cover for a record label and, if you are good and lucky, get more work from other record companies on the basis of your work.

Following the example of Job Wouters (a.k.a. Letman), who almost exclusively creates posters in handmade-style typography, we see that one can hit one's niche by being extraordinarily good at one very particular thing. In his ongoing experimentation with letters and composition he remains highly recognizable and that is why clients approach him:

"Ideally they don't know exactly what they want, but trust my skills and approach. Of course these people have seen my site, and know more or less what to expect."

Even so he's not keen on repeating solutions for different contexts; he likes his work to be alive, and wants to keep developing it and growing with it. Apart from his website, he gets through to people by networking in Amsterdam and also has an agent who helps him sell his work.

Job Wouters, Yvo Spey: Veenfabriek pakt uit (de Veenfabriek, 2007)

Job Wouters (Letman)
Freelancer
Amsterdam, The Netherlands
He is cuckoo about letters, and his designs are transparent, leaving room to breathe. Those letters are curious and have things to say, they are so clear it tickles your eye and make you blink. His handmade style fits the boundaries of typography like a universe on itself by lashing out to illustration, graffiti, and graphic design. They are clear and cunning, together they stand strong.
www.letman.com

Job Wouters, Yvo Spey: Wows & Ows (Amsterdam Weekly, 2006)

Job Wouters: Mighty Nights (MRKMLN group, 2007)

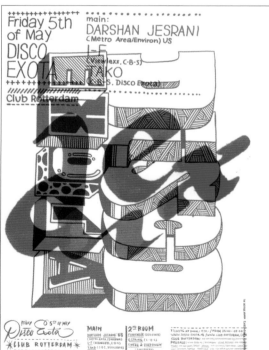

Disciplines

In order to organize and communicate their message, designers arrange colors, shapes, images, type, materials, and textures with the goal of generating aesthetically pleasing communication material. You can learn the basic principles of graphic design in school or on your own (with a little help from friends and/or books).

The avenue you take depends largely on the specialty you choose. Some design specialties require the use of more technical knowledge; as a book designer (who typically focuses on choosing typography, making mockups, picking the paper and monitoring the actual print process) you'll need to be trained in printing techniques, binding, and color calibration. Others, such as advertising, imply a better understanding of society and consumer trends, as well as group dynamics.

You might know how to design a font but that does not mean you are an expert at branding, although it is an essential part of a company's visual identity. Advertising involves not only adapting ads to different formats, but also knowing how each instance fits in a larger scale—which involves complex team mechanics, and is a science unto itself.

The results of our survey show most designers tend to span a multiplicity of disciplines, as they prefer variety, learning and improving their skills and feeling creatively challenged by unfamiliar tasks. To some, specialization is to be avoided because a specialist market is, by definition, smaller and there might not be enough specialist work to go around. Others think doing the same thing all the time is boring.

People seem rarely to start out as graphic designers with a specialization in mind, as their interests are broad and manifold. One day you want to design your own letterhead, another a poster, and maybe a website at some point to show off your print work. You can and should do anything you want at the beginning of your career, while you are still looking for something to call your own. Try everything on for size. You can always switch to another discipline later, in case you become fed up with the limitations your first choice imposes on your work.

Eva, Conny, and Sebastien at Troika share a mutual love of simplicity, playfulness, and an essential desire for provocation:

Troika
Art and design studio
London
Founded in 2003, by Conny Freyer, Eva Rucki and Sebastien Noel, Troika focuses on the creative use of technology to develop projects both engaging and demanding to the user, where design and information never stray far from each other. Their projects development processes are born out of a mutual love for simplicity, playfulness, and an essential desire for provocation.
www.troika.uk.com

Troika: SMS Guerrilla Projector (self-initiated and for Warner Music, 2003-2005)

"Whilst the work of our studio spans various disciplines from graphics over products to installations, a lot of the themes—like the creative use of technology and cross-fertilization between the art and design disciples—are reoccurring subjects. We used to wonder if it was necessary to confine ourselves to one category, to fit in one clearly labeled box, in order for people—and clients specifically—to understand what we were capable of. It turned out that people were excited rather than confused by the different areas we cover. Now, we just enjoy the fact that we have created an environment for ourselves in which we can engage with a variety of different subjects. The different expertise each team member brings to the table is one of our most valuable assets and inspirations and we believe that a multidisciplinary team is fruitful ground for innovation."

Finding your specialization can be like going through a crush. You stumble upon one while doing something else and it sticks to you like glue. You cannot get your crush out of your mind and you cannot think about anything else but this special little person. Some people choose a specialization hoping to work for a particular company or brand, aware that a certain skillset is required for those positions. Others choose one because designing motion graphics for MTV titles, for example, is trendy at that particular moment, which is not the best way to succeed in your work considering fashions come and go. Since your designs need to fulfill a purpose for the end user you need to be able to define and understand your target audience as well as how they will interact with your work. You need to get to know the medium intimately, its possibilities and limitations, technically as well as creatively.

Depending on the field you choose you will have to collaborate with other professionals and also get to know their work and how to get the most out of their expertise. Sometimes you will work with illustrators or photographers, other times with engineers or production artists, as well as the many others you will surely come across in your career. You will need to be aware of who is who, and what his or her role is in the design process.

Different disciplines sometimes also imply different hierarchies. In most design careers, you will move up the ladder from intern or junior-level designer to senior-level designer, art director, or creative director, based on the quality of your work, leadership abilities, and your overall experience. Each specialty is unique in its requirements, so your portfolio should reflect your competence in the area you have chosen to pursue.

Troika: Listening Post (Science Museum, London, 2008), photo © Ben Rubin, Mark Hansen 2008

Advertising

Many graphic designers work in advertising. This is a dynamic and creative field, and if you're on board with the right agency you can also benefit financially (compared with designers working in other disciplines). Advertising budgets have increased dramatically in recent years. In 2006, spending on advertising was estimated at $155 billion in the U.S.[3] and $385 billion worldwide.[4] The latter is expected to exceed $500 billion by 2010.

In contrast to all the other areas of expertise we will cover, advertising is a form of communication that combines many disciplines. You need to be able to stretch advertising concepts over a range of media, taking into considera-

tion the brand character and the audience targeted for consuming the particular product or service. A brand is a collection of images, ideas, and experiences that represent a certain product or a producer. In other words, it is the philosophy behind any product. You are usually given this set of standards, which are not just visual, but also contextual. For instance, Nike is represented by its logo, otherwise known as "the swoosh," the slogan, "Just do it" and dynamic photos of people... well, just doing it. They are achieving heroic accomplishments of which you, too, are capable, wearing snug sports clothes with the same brand idea. If you wear it, you can do it. Identification is the name of the game. I wear it, therefore I am it.

To please your advertising clients, you need to stay within their brand standards. No matter how limiting it seems, there are ways around it. Commercial advertising is constantly reinventing itself and discovering new channels through which to reach customers.

To name but a few:

POS or "point of sale" advertising is just what it says—designed to grab the attention of customers in the place where the product is sold. Many applications exist with imaginative names

Gui Borchert, R/GA: Sneaker Restoration
(Nike Restoration, 2005)

like "shelftalker," "ceiling hanger," "floor sticker," and so on.

Be creative! Invent some of your own!

OOH stands for "out of home." Outdoor advertising includes your average billboards, in various shapes and formats, backlit or just plain and massive in scale.

Print can be newspapers, magazines, poster ads, brochures, and such.

TVC are television commercials that with the advent of TiVo and other cable TV services are losing ground and moving to the Internet in the form of viral video.

Guerrilla is all nonconventional media. This has gained in popularity in the past decade as it involves everything on which a logo can be printed, or even insinuate some association with your brand: skywriting, human directional, towncriers, sides of buses or airplanes ("logojets"), taxicab doors, musical stage shows, subway platforms and trains, elastic bands on disposable diapers, stickers on apples in supermarkets, shopping cart handles, and the backs of event tickets and supermarket receipts.

Any place an "identified" sponsor pays to deliver their message through a medium is advertising.

Web advertising and social media advertising at the moment is still a young market with a lot of promise. They offer advertisers the ability to take advantage of the demographic information the user has provided.[4]

Print

Graphic design used to be the applied art of designing for print exclusively, before other mediums came into the picture. The field of print design is vast, covering basically any printed matter from business cards to magazines, posters and billboards to cd covers. Unless you decide to dedicate yourself to making pop-up books, the industry involves a two dimensional medium that has its limitations. The more you get to know these limits, the more you become aware of the infinite possibilities they contain.

Apart from mastering the written and unwritten rules of placing the elements of your design within a grid, you need to get to know your way around the printing process—from picking the right paper to color separation. The better you control the process of reproduction, the truer your results will be to your initial idea.

Human directional used to be people wearing signs, like sandwich men of old, but now they wear branded uniforms or even have logos tattooed on them. Twenty-year-old Andrew Fischer sold advertising space on his forehead for $37,375 to the company SnoreStop through an auction on eBay and a swimsuit model Shaune Bagwell, managed to sell ad-space on her chest for $15,099 to the Internet casino GoldenPalace.com.

Town criers were the first news services. The technique was used to sell papers in the old days, as well, and now amounts to *voicevertising*, as in the example of Floyd Hayes, who put his voice up for sale on eBay, promising to shout out a brand name as loud as possible every 15 minutes for an entire week, no matter what location or situation.

Mario Hugo: Hanne Hukkelberg (Propellor Recordings/Non-Format, 2007)

Illustration

It is safe to say that most designers at some point flirt with illustration. Whether it's intended to clarify complicated concepts or objects, or serve as a more abstract detail in your piece, designers become drawn to illustration because not only can it enhance their work by providing a visual representation that corresponds to the content, but also it can also give a more personal touch to a piece. Unfortunately, great illustrators are being ousted from jobs as readymade stock illustrations flood the market. An increasing number of illustrators are facing the decision of either retaining their artistic standards (and, hence, fees), but at the risk of securing fewer jobs, or submitting a large volume of spot illustrations to stock agencies at reduced fees.

Identity

Designing visual identities involves the design and application of logos as well as the creation of visual standard manuals (also known as style guides) for other designers. Visual identity should provide visibility and render the given organization recognizable. It is vital that people know a company exists, and remember its name and core business. Good visual identity should allow employees and clients alike to identify with the company of their choice.

Klas Ernflo: B/W Drawings (self-initiated, 2007)

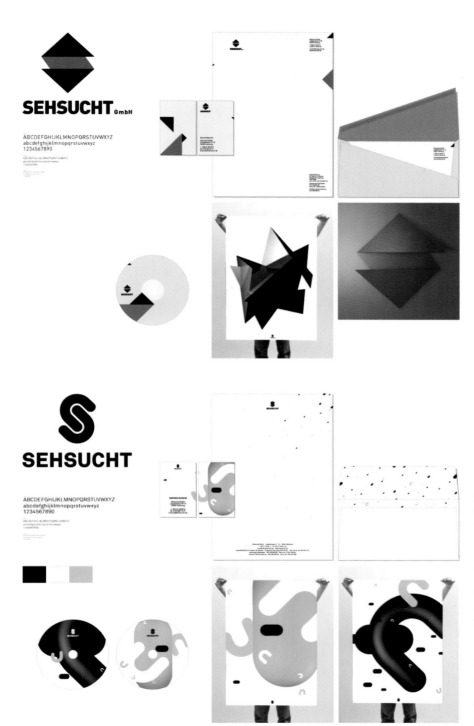

Axel Peemöller: Corporate Identity Concepts (Sehsucht, 2008)

Richard Niessen: Lepidoptera Domestica (Manon van Kouswijk, 2007)

The main elements of branding/visual identity are logos, fonts, color schemes, symbols, ideas, and even personality. In its essence a brand is a set of emotions and the associations it evokes in the end user.

Books/Editorials

It is not clear which medium employs the most graphic designers, but it would be safe to assume that magazines and newspapers offer employment opportunities to a large chunk of graphic designers today, divvied between their promotional and editorial departments.

An editorial designer specializing in the layout and composition of books, magazines or newspapers must take into consideration available printing processes and his or her target audience to be able to deliver the content message more efficiently. All elements of design text, layout as well as internal and external graphics, should be in accordance with the publication concept, based on where they are applied. Pay special attention to the outside front cover and the outside back cover, as these create first impressions, often include advertisements, and, hence, may increase the

sales of the unit in question. Think about how many people actually judge a book by its cover.

When designing any of these materials, you should first think of their content, as different applications and different genres have their own specific formats, compositions, and hierarchies. Take into consideration your target audience as well, as your layout should be based on the social and cultural values of your readers. Even in graphic design, there is a difference between layouts for housewives and teenagers. If you can't connect with your audience, you might just want to keep your day job.

Last, but not least, pay attention to your competition. Analyze them well so you can establish your product better, based on what you learned from their successes and mistakes.

Know the difference between a front cover and the dust jacket. Spread your page and get your guns out. Face the canons of page construction.

Typography

In light of the enduring power of the written word, typography is everywhere you turn. It gives appeal and character to text. Every designer must learn which type to choose, how to use it and when to emphasize it in line with the content. If you, for example, design signalization for public transport, picking the wrong type might lead to a grotesque accident.

Typography is an art form in its own right, as good fonts are difficult to come by (or are too expensive to buy).

When choosing a font, a designer must think about legibility and avoid creating the kind of visual chaos that ensues when one uses too many different types of letters.

Typography should address the visual problems presented by the length of the text, improving the overall readability. For example, longer texts need more regular characters, and decorative ones can be splashed out on titles and excerpts and captions. Always bear in mind the link between your typography and the nature of the publication you are using it for, as it should make visual sense.

Copland

AABBCCDEFGGHIJKKLVMNNOO
PQRRSTUUVWVXYZZ
0123456 789
ÆŒ(.,;:)Ù&?!

Helfin regular

abcdefghijklmnopqrstuvwxyz
ABCDEFFGGHIJKLMNOPQRRSTUVWWXYZ
0123456789   &?!/âãáæéè êœç(.,;:)

Helgras regular

abcdefghijklmnopqrstuvwxyz
ABCDEFFGGHIJKLMNOPQRRSTUVWXYZ
0123456789   &?!/âãáæéèêœç(.,;:)

Sylvia Torunerie, Gilles Poplin: Original font types (self-initiated, 2004-2006)

Packaging

In many senses packaging has become as important as the product itself. In the process, you have to bear in mind that you are preparing goods for transport, warehousing, logistics, sale, and end use, all in one go.

The role of packaging design is to contain, protect, inform, and, finally, sell the product contained within the packaging. It should also pay attention to the brand character, as mentioned in the advertising chapter.

Paperjam Design: Healthy Hounds packaging (Paddy Paws, 2007)

Web/Interface/Interactive

Web design is a process of conceptualizing, planning, modeling, and executing electronic media content delivery via the Internet—or, to be more precise, through a Web browser. It has two ends; the front-end and the back-end, and the designer's job is mainly at the front, while programmers take care of the dirty work. In this case, making the design look good means knowing the limitations of your medium.

Web design differs from print design in its very basic functionality. Printed materials are static, viewed selectively, whereas Web pages are animated and interactive.

Interface design and the information architecture behind it jointly work together to create a user experience that is as painless and fast as possible. Jakob Nielsen, a usability guru who Web designers love to hate, sums it up in one sentence: "Users visiting a new site spend an average of 30 seconds on the homepage and less than 2 minutes on the entire site before deciding to abandon it. They spend a bit more time if they decide to stay on a site, but still only 4 minutes on average. If they have to spend 15 of their 30 seconds figuring out which link to click on your home page, you've probably lost them". [5]

Designing an interface is a challenging task, as you need to be able to work from the point of view of an average user, taking into account usability and information architecture. Poorly thought out interfaces could cripple usability, as the average user often will not take the time to figure out the navigation of a site.

Building the rest of the website means working with programmers and content managers. Once that is accomplished, you have a website—a collection of electronic files residing on one or more Web servers and on display to the end user. They can be static or dynamic.

Renda Morton/*Rumors:* Website for architecture firm Interloop (Interloop, 2007)

Umberto Eco (January 5, 1932) is an Italian medievalist, semiotician, philosopher, literary critic, and novelist who holds over thirty honorary doctorates from various academic institutions worldwide and has founded *Versus: Quaderni di studii semiotici*, an influential semiotic journal and a publication platform for many scholars whose work is related to signs and signification.

Troika: All the Time in the World (Artwise Curators, 2008)
photo © Alex Delfanne/Artwise Curators 2008

Signage

Signs vary depending on their usage. They employ various symbols, icons, logos, colors, and shapes for easy identification and have kept their primary communications role since the dawn of graphic design. Umberto Eco summed it up nicely, saying that a sign is everything that stands for something else, based on an agreed social convention. Be sensitive to cultural contexts as well as how an audience will receive your particular sign or sign system. If the interpretation of the message—that is, the meaning—of the sign is not clear to the recipient, then it does not work.

Trends or Style

Being on the constant lookout for a project that makes your portfolio shine does not really make for a creative process. Competition surrounds you. With every magazine you look at and every website you frequent, you wonder: are they all a step ahead of you? It always seems other people have better clients, more time, and consistently come up with better solutions, which creates an altogether new kind of pressure.

At the same time, trends in graphic design are changing quicker than you can flip through the pages of the latest issue of your favorite cutting-edge graphic design magazine.

Between the pressures of working at deft speed, ensuring your clients get what they want, paying your bills, and enjoying what you do, it isn't difficult to fall into the trap of feeling that it is difficult to create good work—especially now that graphic design has become such an integral part of consumer culture.

The Good, the Bad and the Ones That Work

Clients perceive design more as a means to an end than as a creative visual solution. For clients, design is a strategic decision; it is the way they present their marketing and communications messages to their own clients. You have to be aware of that. It might look great, but if you used eight-point type for a target audience over forty years of age, they might not be able to read it. In that case, design overtakes, rather than reinforces, the message. Too many designers are only interested in what they want to create and not in what the client wants to achieve. Sometimes it is not all about the image, it is about substance in your design, as Sheila Levrant de Bretteville put it in the title of the poster she created in 1970 for the then-new California Institute of the Arts in Valencia: *Taste and Style Aren't Enough.*

There is a difference between creating art and having artistic sensibility while designing. One is about self-expression and communication for the sake of one's self; the other focuses on the client's goals, and communicating in a way that the audience can understand.

That is what you should do—solve problems. Magnify the invisible stuff from the visual noise that surrounds us. Problem solving is a liberating art form. No one can teach you how to do it.

Even when we design, for example, a centerpiece flower arrangement for a formal table setting, we cannot design without inherently thinking and working in a problem-solving mode. Through both design and problem solving, we are focused on "changing existing situations into preferred ones."

Thinking about the final product before you spend time thinking about the details is fun and easy, as it has no limitations. You can have the greatest ideas in the history of design, but they are worth next to nothing if they do not do what your client wants, or if you cannot persuade your client that is what he or she needs. Sometimes you should not give them what they want, but what they need. This usually happens if the client is inexperienced in or misinformed about your field of work. Work for the client. Don't make the client work for you.

Designing should lead to purposeful and practical outcomes. As creative as your job can be, you need to think it through to achieve good results. You need to learn the rules, forget the rules,

turn the questions upside down, start at the end and move toward the beginning. Do not fall in love with your projects. Learn to kill them if they do not do their job.

Judging the quality of graphic design is subjective. What is the criteria of what we're looking for anyways? Is good equal to memorable? Visible? Straightforward? Transformative? Good design speaks clearly and concisely about something you understand on a subconscious level before you have time to digest information. If you felt invited to look, or encouraged to continue, that is good. If you did not feel the magic by looking at it, it just might not be that good.

Doing Your Own Thing

To create is to exercise power over oneself and over one's environment. You want to say: I existed, I made this. This is my footprint on the moon. Then again, an act of personal creation does not give you any guidelines to how good your work really is. Aesthetic questions are personal for every designer. So is style.

Many young designers mistake style for design, so we will try to differentiate them here. Design communicates on every level, while style communicates just stylishness. Certain established styles are easily linked to brand values (like the link between graffiti wildstyle writing with hip-hop youth fashion brands) and are therefore used as important elements of design, but when style is king, design confuses users and hurts the client.

There are people who have made a name for themselves through a particular, oft-copied style, and clients go to their shops because that is what they want. How long can they last? If dazzle and flash are the values of today's society, how many rehashes of the same work will keep the audience mesmerized?

Working as a designer usually means being creative in a particular area of expertise, but it also means having a task to accomplish on time under conditions given by a client (some of which he is not even aware), and for many designers that translates into a restraining order on creativity. The formulaic approach to design from days of yore is no more. The needs of your clients differ as much as that of their audiences. Design now is more than just a sum of fonts, colors, and graphical elements. It has moved into the conceptual realms of art, but it still has to be accessible and understandable to its audiences. It has to work for your client.

Who do you appreciate more in the end, the graphic designers themselves or their style?

At a certain point in their career, some designers choose a technical field to master, while other develop a recognizable style in order to be more competitive. We could call it their consumer benefit, a brand value. A distinctive and special style is something that is easily recognized and

Fiodor Sumkin
Ilustrator and designer
Amsterdam, The Netherlands
Opera78 is the creative studio run by Amsterdam-based illustrator Fiodor Sumkin. His work is a synergistic blend of lovingly crafted pen and ink watercolors with biting social commentary. His designed type and fresh style of illustration complement each other beautifully.
opera78.com

Fiodor Sumkin: Corny (self-initiated, 2008)

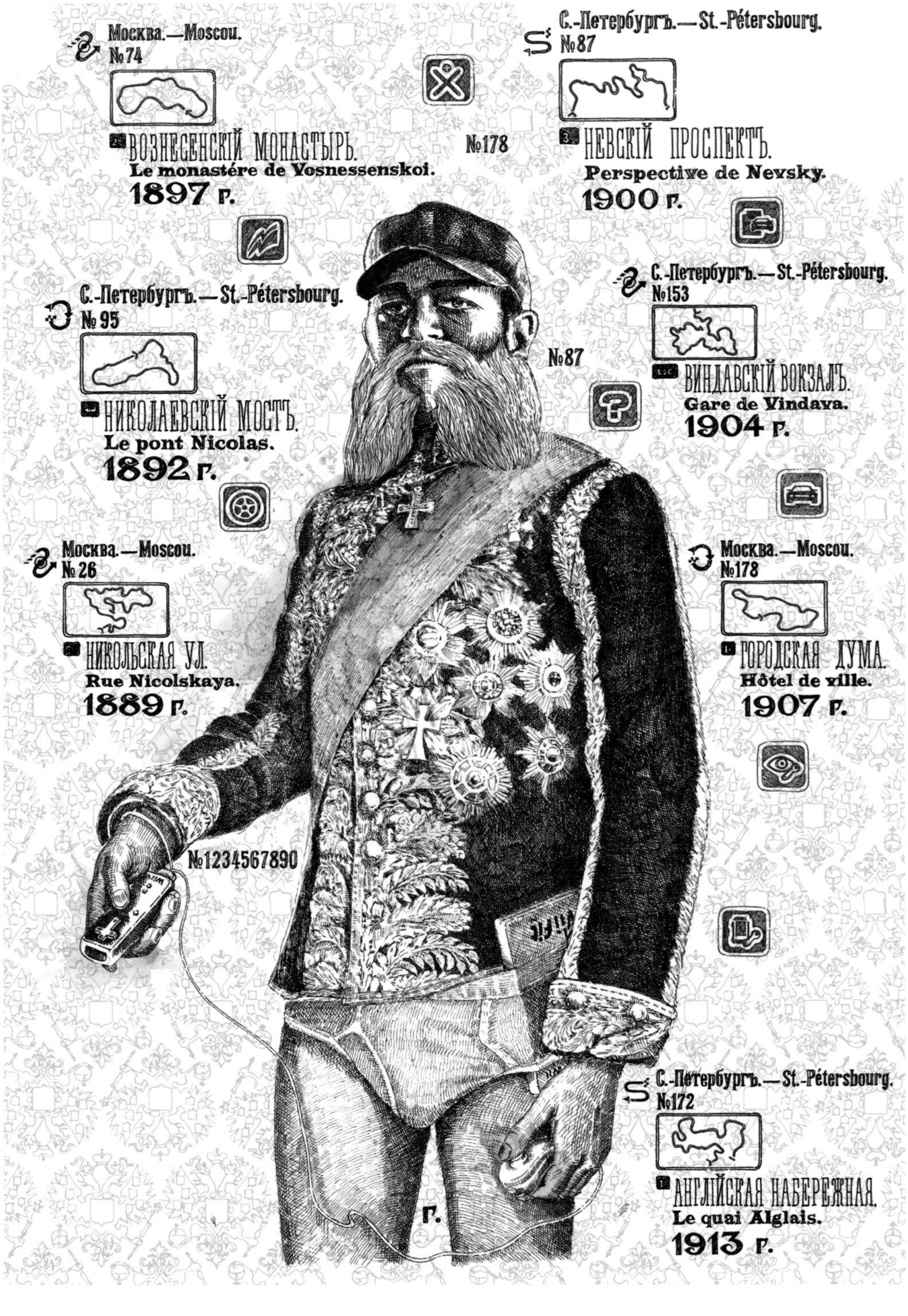

Москва.—Moscou.
№74

ВОЗНЕСЕНСКІЙ МОНАСТЫРЬ.
Le monastère de Vosnessenskoï.
1897 г.

№178

С.-Петербургъ.—St.-Pétersbourg.
№87

НЕВСКІЙ ПРОСПЕКТЪ.
Perspective de Nevsky.
1900 г.

С.-Петербургъ.—St.-Pétersbourg.
№95

НИКОЛАЕВСКІЙ МОСТЪ.
Le pont Nicolas.
1892 г.

№87

С.-Петербургъ.—St.-Pétersbourg.
№153

ВИНДАВСКІЙ ВОКЗАЛЪ.
Gare de Vindava.
1904 г.

Москва.—Moscou.
№26

НИКОЛЬСКАЯ УЛ.
Rue Nicolskaya.
1889 г.

Москва.—Moscou.
№178

ГОРОДСКАЯ ДУМА.
Hôtel de ville.
1907 г.

№1234567890

С.-Петербургъ.—St.-Pétersbourg.
№172

АНГЛІЙСКАЯ НАБЕРЕЖНАЯ.
Le quai Alglais.
1913 г.

Г.

Fiodor Sumkin: The Tsar of Wii (Self-initiated, 2008)

great styles are often copied. In a way, specific style are themselves a brand, and good brands are marketable as long as their appeal to the general public is present.

When Fiodor Sumkin started his career as an illustrator he didn't think much about balancing his style with the client's needs:

"I knew precisely what I was interested in doing and how to do it. I try to create every new project so that it is different from the previous ones. I follow new trends in design and use my intuition. This helps me to know what will come in the air in the next few months or half a year. I am always true to my style. There are always some rules I follow. For example, I will never make vector or 3D illustrations. I draw all my images with a gel pen on simple A4 paper."

For Fiodor it works perfectly fine since he keeps on reinventing himself and already became an icon in the world of illustration. But for many others, especially when we look at it from a graphic design angle, the trouble with style is that it eventually goes out of style, even while it takes a significant investment of time to develop a signature style. As

with any field there are those style mavericks who keep pushing the limits of how far one particular style can last.

Sylvia Tournerie doesn't think through style.

"What's interesting is the idea that with the exact same subject, format, and tools, every graphic designer will do something different. When you are working, searching, there is a time when you feel something, something that says *this* is interesting, and no matter if it's good or not, this is a personal and unique feeling.

"And then when you work to make your image or layout in its final version you know that it's the composition that 'suits' you. But you also know that your neighbor would have probably made the text smaller and placed it more on the left because that would have 'suited' him."

No matter if you decide to be a one-man band or an expert in designing consumer packaged goods, you need to be open to ideas and fill your head with ideas and references. The more sensitive you become to the world around you, the better you will do.

Sylvia Tournerie
Graphic designer
Paris, France
Sylvia has been freelancing since 1996. She specialises in music, art, and culture, and has a passion for typography. Her clients range from Andrea Crews and Cosmo Vitelli to Mirwais and Levi's.
www.sylvia-tournerie.com

Sylvia Tournerie: Prototypes (Boxson/Universal, 2007)

Sylvia Tournerie: Prototypes (Boxson / Universal, 2007)

34.DESIGN UND ZEIT
I'VE HEARD ABOUT

Entretien avec François Roche

A VILLE

A POLIN NUM RIQUE

MO N GRATE

N ALGUE

20.DOSSIER
RICHARD WRIGHT
A REBOURS

Every Time Someone Says "Ethics" a Designer Loses His Wings

Design ethics is a slippery slope. Even though graphic design originates from the dawn of consumer culture, there is more to it than shopping and advertising. The first official attempt to re-radicalize design was called *First Things First* manifesto, published in 1964 by Ken Garland, in which 400 graphic designers railed against consumerism, hoping to start up a new design theory based on a humanist dimension. This manifesto was later appropriated and updated by *Adbusters* in 1999, under the name *First Things First 2000* manifesto, and signed by thirty-three important international graphic design figures.

Some choose to live by it, others ignore it.

Regardless of your views on whether design should or should not be value-free, we cannot help but feel that nowadays outside of design institutions and perhaps some schools with courses that tackle these particular issues, the word ethics seems to be frowned upon, akin to a moralizing phrase uttered by your mother or an old teacher. Most people seem to be more interested in talking about salaries than principles, as if ethics were something silly and passé, with no place in our everyday professional lives. To be fair, it is often the case that working designers, as opposed to teaching designers, are inundated by the burden of their everyday workload and often do not have the luxury of time to ruminate on issues—ethics, for example—rendered academic by the sheer pace of their profession.

Sometimes you are told that you can and need to make a difference in the world as a designer, others and you warn against getting too carried away with principles since you cannot change humanity with every logo or trivial flyer you make.

First Things First, 1964, Published by Ken Garland, Printed by Goodwin Press Ltd

Either way, you should be proud of each new effort and each new creation, but by serving commercial interests you are bound to face some, perhaps, unpleasant decisions. What you do might be pleasing to the eye, but it needs to be grounded in principle.

As Dan Saffer paraphrased his professor Richard Buchanan in his essay *Ethics in Design:*

"Principles are what organize. They ground us in organizations and in the world. Principles are values, which are facts, which equal status in the world. It is a fact that people value things. People will die for their values. Navigating remarkably conflicting values is one of the central problems of design. It is all about what is the right thing to do, and not just technically."[6]

Saving the World

Most of the time, commissioned work has nothing to do with saving the world or making statements as a graphic designer. Many designers still feel the need to express themselves beyond the brief, and in those cases self-initiated projects serve as a great outlet.

Amelia Roberts confessed she had the great opportunity as a student to do many self-initiated projects:

"I have had a huge amount of freedom in creating and communicating issues that are of interest to me. Graphic design is a brilliant outlet that potentially allows ideas to be shown to a large range of different people. I do think that it is important that a designer's voice can be heard as long as it is used responsibly and is in keeping with the client's requirements."

Her experiences as a young designer are largely without conflict, and clients usually accept her ideas for using recycled paper and more "environment-friendly" techniques. She believes that the larger challenges are to come, as clients become larger and pressures increase.

The tale of Ernst Bettler's design work for the pharmaceutical company Pfäfferli + Huber in 1958 leaves her especially inspired. And though the story is a hoax, Amelia cannot help but think what potential design can hold.

Ernst Bettler was invented in an article Cristopher Wilson published in *Dot Dot Dot* magazine, in 2000. According to the article, Bettler was supposed to design posters for a Swiss pharmaceutical company called Pfäfferli + Huber (P+H). The company's alleged involvement with Nazi concentration camp experiments provoked Bettler to

Amelia Roberts
Graduate
London
Having just graduated from university she is looking forward to continuing to explore the different avenues and aspects of graphic design. She hopes to travel and keep on developing and learning how to communicate ideas in new and stimulating ways; it is important for her to be inspired from all different aspects of life.
www.ameliaroberts.com

Amelia Roberts: Global Warming (self-initiated, 2008)

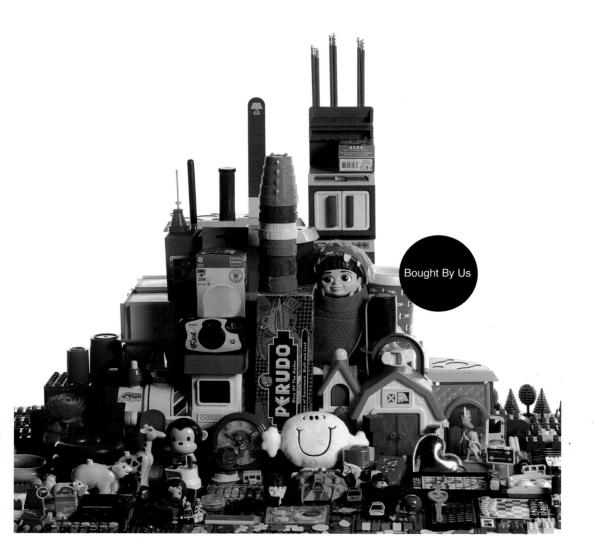

Bought By Us

create posters whose abstract compositions could be read as capital letters spelling out "N-A-Z-I" when displayed in sequence. Supposedly these posters ruined the company in a matter of weeks.

This graphic design fairy tale, outlining the power the medium has as the message was well received and subsequently retold by *Adbusters* as "one of the greatest design interventions on record." Michael Johnson called Bettler the "founding father of the 'culture-jamming' form of protest."

Andy Crewdson exposed the Bettler hoax in a 2002 entry in the blog Lines and Splines. In an article in the February 2003 issue of *Eye* magazine, Rick Poynor analyzed the life that the Bettler hoax took since its original publication, having been quoted and hailed in the design community as a testament to design's power to change things. In actuality, it was a subtle reminder of the limitations of design's power to change things.

Or can it?

Saving Yourself

As a graphic designer you will build an infinite array of relationships, and even though some are more tangible than others, you should be aware of these intricacies and how what you do affects things on a larger scale.

Being mediators between your clients and the public carries a certain responsability. Let's say you need to portray a message to an audience through which they connect a company to its consumers; this means you are responsible for the way a company or a product is perceived, but also for the transmitted information not being adverse toward the audience in any way.

Although much of what follows implies common sense, there is no harm in stating what seems obvious.

Protecting your client's interests is a part of your job description, but presenting false or misleading information should not be. You are responsible not only to your client, but also to the public, your colleagues, the people with whom you work, and, ultimately, yourself. We could say "microethics" considers individuals and internal relations of the profession while "macroethics" refers to our collective social responsibility.

Before starting a new project ask yourself: is it harmful to the public or is it discriminating against anyone in any way? Try being sensitive to your entire audience. If you are not familiar with the cultural context, familiarize yourself with it.

Respect your colleagues. They are in the same boat as you are. Being competitive is perfectly fine as long as you're fair. If you have collaborated with another designer or a studio on a project, be sure to assign credit accordingly. Be honest when you present yourself and your capabilities; filling up your CV with falsehoods (projects you didn't accomplish, schools you didn't attend) or embellishments will backfire on you sooner or later. React if you see your client is providing you with material for which he owns no rights, or has unsettled matters with another designer while asking you to work on the same project.

Nurture a professional and respectful relationship with the hand that feeds you; respect deadlines and the contract you sign with your client, inform him properly on timings, production methods, and budgets. Be mindful of potential conflicts of interest when working simultaneously on projects for different clients.

You will inevitably land in various delicate situations and there is no point in trying to address them all here, but you get the idea. Following these guidelines does not make you a hippie dreamer with no sense of business. It makes you a decent person (to work with).

Pfäfferli+Huber Pharmaceuticals, poster attributed to Ernst Bettler, 1959 [7]

HAVE YOU HAD FORMAL EDUCATION IN GRAPHIC DESIGN?

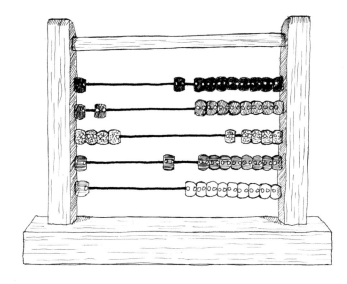

No = 18.3%

Yes, vocational degree = 14.2%

Yes, BFA = 36.5%

Yes, MFA = 6.9%

Yes, PHD = 1.5%

Yes, doctorate = 0.7%

Other = 21.9%

WHAT EXPERIENCES DID YOU HAVE WITH YOUR SCHOOL?

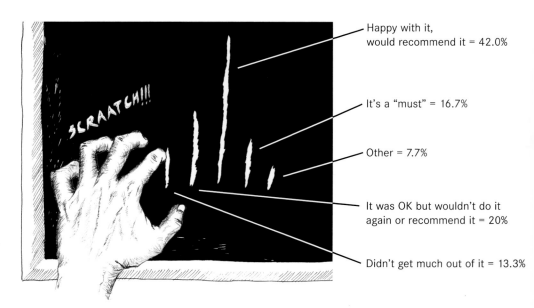

Happy with it, would recommend it = 42.0%

It's a "must" = 16.7%

Other = 7.7%

It was OK but wouldn't do it again or recommend it = 20%

Didn't get much out of it = 13.3%

EDUCATION

There is no universally perfect educational system or teacher capable of giving you all the knowledge and experiences you need. So even if you have graduated from a school, or are about to choose one, your education will be entirely up to you since the only measure of good education is self-motivation and personal involvement.

If you think this is an excuse not to go to school, think again. Some schools might be old fashioned and boring but they can give you a head start and a good foundation on which to build. Do you wish to learn more about the craft or the industry? Perhaps you want to specialize in something?

Well don't worry too much, because school is only the beginning of your education anyway. There are internships, seminars, workshops, books, and a ton of work experience ahead of you. As you live and learn, you make choices about whether you want to learn in a classroom or through experience. Even the most talented self-taught designers out there needed to work hard to learn the tricks of the trade.

Good to Know Is Difficult to Learn

How important is formal education? Do you really need it, or can graphic design be mastered intuitively? What do you learn in school, and is it worth the money? Can't everyone just do it? I've got the software!

Well you should know better than that by now. Most graphic designers gained knowledge of the subject at hand either through classical formal education aimed at imparting theoretical and some practical knowledge and developing your intellectual capacities, or through long, painful hours of self-improvement via books, the Internet, magazines, friends, and other resources.

It's not only about guidance, but also about learning how to reason with the rest of the world about what exactly makes design special and worth more than just another pretty picture; you need to be able to communicate your ideas in writing, visually, and verbally. Ideally, formal education should give you some guidance in these directions.

Times have changed. A degree is required for some entry-level design positions, but in order to get a job your portfolio and CV are far more important than the training you've received. On the other hand, one of the benefits of a good school is that your portfolio should be more impressive and diverse than if you had chosen the DIY route.

Why Go to School?

A design degree means at least a(nother) few years of education, and who wants that?

For one, going to school makes you learn the "boring" historical context behind your little colors, shapes, and grids you would otherwise take for granted. A font is just another font, unless you know the story of its making. It allows you to put things into perspective.

A proper school can give you a good starting point by surrounding you with colleagues with whom you can exchange your ideas and share your miseries; it will accustom you to the continuity of working and handling multiple projects. The right balance between theory and practice will make it easier to apply for internships, find your place in the profession, and land your first job.

For Roanne Adams, formal training meant the opportunity to work straight out of school, and now she is running her own studio.

"Going through the training has provided me with a way to think and apply my knowledge to my projects. There is a kind of thinking and process that is associated with a graphic design education that I would have not obtained on my own."

Even so, she had met some designers who never studied graphic design yet were quite talented:

"Most of them studied art or architecture, so they had a certain tool to start out with. I don't think this route is for everyone. I think it takes an exceptional talent to be able to master style and technique without training prior to entering the work world. I do think that learning on the job is a huge component to a designer's talent. Interning can be a great alternative to studying in school."

She found that she didn't learn much about the industry until she was out in the working world:

"When I was in school I was much more interested in the craft, which I think is what design school is for. It's the only time that you can really focus on your craft and fine-tune your style.

"When I decided to go freelance, though, my lack of knowledge about

the industry became very apparent. I didn't know much about print production, timing, budgets, proposals, pitches, etc. because I worked with teams at Wolff Olins that took care of all of that for me. As a designer, I think it is incredibly important to understand the craft as well as the business no matter where you work. I luckily kept good relationships with my co-workers and teachers so all my questions were answered. I also bought a bunch of books on how to run a design studio and how to create budgets."

Roanne Adams
Graphic design and art direction studio
New York
Roanne Adams runs a multidisciplinary design studio in TriBeCa. She is devoted to building iconic and compelling experiences for brands and nonprofits. Specializing in brand revitalization for ailing brands and developing the right look and feel for new brands, Roanne also brings the know-how of maintaining the glow for those who have found the right formula.
www.roanneadams.com

Creative direction: Roanne Adams/design: Tiffany Malakooti: Mathew Cerletty artist book (Rivington Arms, 2007)

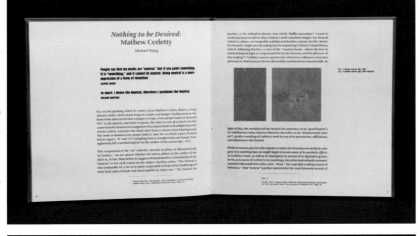

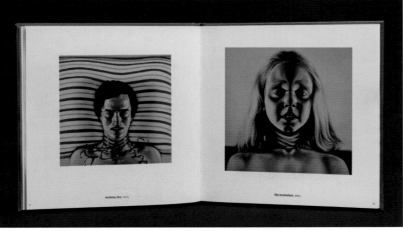

Creative direction: Roanne Adams/design: Tiffany Malakooti: Mathew Cerletty artist book (Rivington Arms, 2007)

Know to Pick What Is Good for You

Before settling on just any school, you should take into consideration your present location and where you want to live, as well as your budget. Programs vary from one school to another; some function in smaller classes and others in large auditoriums. You know what feels best for you. And think about your future, as well. Where do you want to be ten years from now?

Roughly base your search for a school on your primary career choice. There are as many schooling options as there are professional angles, from technical to private art schools.

Universities or four-year colleges are probably the best choice if you want a complete arts education for your graphic design needs. From these you receive a BS (bachelor of science) or BA (bachelor of arts) degree. Such schools give you a broad and well-rounded education, but your design programs might not be as comprehensive as those in art schools.

Institutes or design schools last for four years as well, but focus intensively on design education, featuring a graphic design major and a department. Here you get a lot less science,

humanities, or social studies, which can be a minus later on, when you start work. You end up with a MFA (master of fine arts) degree in some cases.

Two-year programs are a lot cheaper and less time consuming. They focus mostly on learning the computer and technical skills necessary to become a production artist (i.e., someone who prepares art for printing). Such programs will not go into much depth on core design fundamentals like color theory or typography.

Yes, perhaps some of those schools are inert in picking up the latest vibes and styles and opportunities, but they give you a good foundation on which to build your career.

Christopher West does not regret his decision to attend a four-year program he found abroad:

"The good thing is that you learn. There are good schools and bad schools and there are good and bad times in your life for learning.

"Art school is an especially tricky thing because it consumes all your energy and time: it can really change your life. I would even go so far as to say that it should change you. It is the

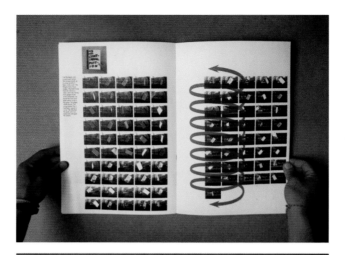

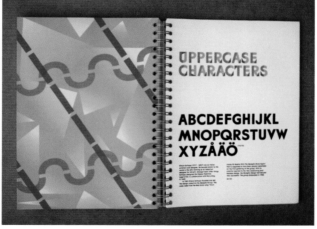

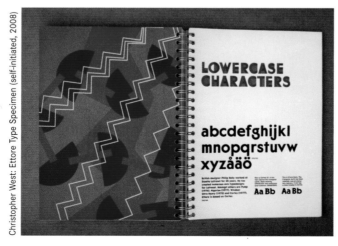

Christopher West: Ettore Type Specimen (self-initiated, 2008)

time when you have a chance to question your choice of profession again and again. It's also a place to meet people, make friends, try, and learn.

"I'm not an autodidact. Even if you are really good at what you do, I still think three to five years in art school can't hurt you. In the best instance you will be forced to solve problems in another way than you are used to. Trying new paths and renewing your thinking is crucial to make interesting stuff."

For him personally it is more important to learn the craft than how to work in the industry:

"The time you have for education is very short, it is precious. I'd rather learn how to refine my work, my thoughts and my ideas, than learn how an ad agency works. I have a whole working-life to get to know 'the industry'."

Some schools prefer to teach visual artists rather than designers by developing their capacities and creativity, focusing on the individual personality of each student. This is done through project-based research in desired fields. Students have to show a high level of involvement with others and with society. Teachers and mentors will nudge them toward conceptual thinking and the creation of their own

language within given fields and techniques with an accent on investigation, experimentation, and authorship.

Other schools are oriented toward design in an entrepreneurial way, which better prepares students for commercial challenges and creative decision making. Courses are taught by established professionals in the field, which opens a broad range of prospective contacts and keeps students current with practices and trends in the industry. Emphasis is on understanding the entirety of the design process from the initial concept to the final product and its marketing.

Christopher West
Student and freelancer
Amsterdam, The Netherlands
Christopher is a graphic designer from Stockholm, Sweden. He is currently studying at Gerrit Rietveld Academie in Amsterdam, scheduled to graduate in 2009. He enjoys doing books and posters and all other kinds of printed matter. He just finished making his first typeface, and plans on doing more. He still plays music.
www.christopherwest.se

Christopher West, Alban Schelbert: The Information Man (self-initiated, 2008)

Last, but not the least, there are schools that teach you project management above all else, preparing you for a global job market and participatory networking.

The world of graphic design is conditioned by software, and understanding how to use certain technologies is important but not crucial. When it comes to selecting a school or a program, focus on finding one that will teach you about design concepts and fundamentals, instead of offering strong grounding in graphic design software (which you can get from tutorials or a good course). The danger is that you might graduate with training in a certain software yet be employed by people who use another.

No matter which direction you choose, your choice is very individual, notes Christopher West:

"It depends on what kind of work you are interested in, how you work, and what kind of work you want to do when you graduate. The school I'm going to fits me perfectly. But it was as much coincidence as planning that made me come here. Even when I started I didn't know what I was getting into. I have a lot of classmates who have tried out two or more schools before finding the right one."

Get ready to be milked though. Once you sit down and add up all the expenses involved in your education (tuition + accommodation + art supplies), you might get discouraged, but do not give up. Instead of getting frightened by the sticker price, try looking into need-based and merit-based scholarships.

Internship

The recurring reason why many people never become students is because they find schools limiting due to a lack of practical work in the curriculum. In other words, schools can give you a solid theory base and exciting projects, but if they are completely out of touch with the industry you might have a difficult time not only finding a job but also actually learning how it's done.

This is not a problem exclusive to new graduates. Most agencies and studios prefer someone experienced, and nowadays, because of office dynamics, there is rarely a good moment to hire someone fresh out of school that the office has to start with from scratch. The odds of arriving during a lull between projects are quite unlikely; you'll always get in mere days before some important deadline.

It's not a must but was really helpful to get a sensible background

Art School was worth it

STILL THERE

i suppose that it is a MUST

Expensive, slightly pointless, but essential

wish I could have gotten more out of it

It was good, but not necessary. I think it depends on the person - some need the school, some can do it on their own.

AWESOME BUT WAAAAY TOO EXPENSIVE

not very good, but meant a lot to me.

SELF-TAUGHT

Though I think each person will take university/college differently, I feel that it's a MUST and wouldn't be the well rounded artist/designer I am without it.

I thought it was ok, but i would love to try it again knowing what i know now.

I WISH I INVESTED MORE IN IT

I think for most that school is an opportunity to learn, develop and experiment. I don't think that it's a necessity to go to art school but it certainly helps. Ultimately though you need to have ideas and you can't learn that.

Would recommend, but it's not for everyone

I LEARNED THROUGH ASKING

I Learned from Tutorials

IT WAS REALLY BAD

IT WAS A MUST

wish I could have done the 4 years degree...

I didn't feel prepared for the workload. The assignments in school where too artistic and not practical enough.

Made the most of a bad situation, got out of it what i put in.

I loved it SO FAR

it was ok, would do it again but wouldn't recommend it.

A VALUABLE LIFE EXPERIENCE BUT WASN'T TAUGHT MUCH OP PRACTICAL USE. CULTURAL SUPPORTING STUDIES WERE BETTER

It was FANTASTIC PLACE for sharing and collaborating

Had some good teachers who helped me see things differently, but generally, school sucked!

I learned how to present myself but not how to make great design. I would recommend recommend it but at a different school

Studying design and art was great and I think all students should study art at some point. However, in my specific case, I would've chosen a different university in a larger city.

Way better than working. Ideas ideas ideas. compared to mac hack. machack. machack. go figure.

Thinking about studying again.

It's what you make of it.

it got me to where I was going

While it's quite common to start contacting studios for internships after getting a degree, some schools include them as a part of their curriculum. You will probably still be in charge of finding the internship and getting the most out of it, but your school will monitor your progress and keep in touch with your supervisors.

Good internships are like good haircuts: easy to spot, but not so easy to come by. Competition for intern positions has become almost as tough as the actual job-hunting. If you impress your employers with your skills and prove you're a valuable team player, an internship can turn into your first job.

Therefore, you need to be serious in your approach; make it personal, treat it as your first job application.

After narrowing down your choice of studios from which you think you can learn the most, contact each one and introduce yourself. Writing an email or a letter is fine as long as you follow up with a phone call. Convince the studio that hiring you as an intern would be mutually beneficial. Send in a portfolio, but be sure to customize it for each studio.

Once you get in, the intensity with which you learn and grow is almost entirely up to you. It might be a bit frustrating for your ego to start at the bottom, but you'll need to bite your tongue and get over it. Be prepared to observe other people doing interesting work even while your own work is less engaging, and remember that you have an obligation to start developing your skills as a designer while you learn.

Actively training an intern takes a lot of time and energy, and most studios will not have time for it. This is where your attitude counts; it will determine the amount and quality of work you do. If you realize you've been sorting mail and making coffee for two weeks now, you should convince them to trust you with more important tasks.

You will probably get paid very little, if anything at all. Remuneration varies depending on the country or studio. Do your best and stay overtime if needed, but avoid being exploited as cheap labor, or fall into the trap of becoming a perpetual intern.

I can teach myself

Now that we've outlined all the positive aspects of formal schooling, we're going to tell you that skipping school can be a legitimate path to success.

The older you get, the younger the new kids on the design block. You know who we mean—those natural-born designers who started doodling at an early age, made flyers for the neighborhood lemonade stand as soon as he could get his hands on some printing gear and knew his fonts before he planted his first kiss.

A good example is Vadik Marmeladov, a twenty-one-year-old from Moscow who taught himself everything he knows.

He jumped right in without any fear and started wheeling and dealing:

"I think learning how to work in the industry is more useful, especially for young minds. I guess I'm the living proof. We have a lot of energy, a lot of ambitions... but we can't speak our minds or really work as team players. We still don't understand clients. We don't know how to start our own business, etc. Learning the craft is a question of experience."

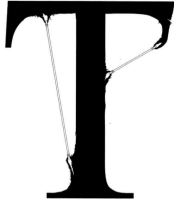

Vadik Marmeladov: T (*Gift Magazine*, 2007)

Vadik Marmeladov
Freelancer
Moscow, Russia
Vadik is a twenty-one-year-old diligent little prince of graphic design and new media art. He's the art director of online *LAM* magazine and recently became the art director of the Russian version of *Dazed & Confused* magazine. Apart from that he's taking care of his own life-long project called Vadik Marmeladov.
www.vadikmarmeladov.com

Vadik Marmeladov: LAM style (*LAM* magazine, 2007)

Vadik Marmeladov: Alchemy (self-initiated, 2008)

He doesn't reject school as an option:

"With a proper education, you won't spend years and years sitting alone at home, trying to create something, figuring out dozens of programs, or wondering why you're doing all this in the first place—and the fact that the money comes eventually. You won't observe the design world through your screen exclusively and read through designers' blogs like I do and you won't speak with your 'graphic designer' friends over ICQ. Instead, you'll have them next to you."

Some of the best designers you know and whose work you admire are actually trained in completely different professions.

Their creative drive made them change their mind at some point and re-evaluate their job situation and make a decision. Some of them live in areas where there are no design schools. Some of them just consider schools boring, old fashioned, and not very inspiring.

Anyone can become an autodidact at any point in life. While some may have been educated in a conventional man- ner in a particular field, they some- times choose to educate themselves in others, often unrelated areas to be able to earn more or give themselves a competitive edge.

If you decide to forego formal educa- tion as a designer, we would advise you find yourself an external neutral eye in the form of a good (critical graphic designer) friend, or even better, a real mentor. This is important for a self- taught designer. Take everything you see, read, and hear, forget about it and be curious about finding other ways to work out a problem.

Sometimes curiosity does not kill the cat, but makes it cooler.

There is, however, a negative side to self-education. Autodidacts may focus too narrowly on a field of interest and neglect whole topics of reading and study in related areas or foundational studies that are required for genuine depth and perspective on a topic. Of course, these are easily remedied with a few more hours of extra reading, so bear in mind that sometimes a little theory and history can open new and exciting horizons.

Peter Mendelsund
Senior designer (Alfred A. Knopf Publisher) and
art director (Vertical)
New York
Peter Mendelsund is a graphic designer, classical pianist, and author of the forthcoming cultural history book *The First Four Notes*. He has jacketed books for almost every major publisher in the United States and abroad, his design work appears in several museum collections, has been featured in numerous magazines, and his editorial illustrations show up frequently in the *New York Times* and other publications.
www.mendelsund.com

Never Too Late

Peter Mendelsund is a senior designer at Knopf, an art director for Vertical, and an independent Japanese-American publisher. A philosophy major, Mendelsund also holds various graduate degrees in music from several conservatories. Also, before becoming a graphic designer he performed, taught, and wrote classical music. When his first child was born, he realized he needed to improve his income and, according to him, graphic design was a natural choice.

His first job was designing CD covers for a small record label with which he had previously recorded. After that he began designing book covers for Vintage and then hard covers for Knopf. The entire transformation from composer to designer transpired in less than a year.

He shares his experiences about starting work as a book cover designer for a major publishing house, virtually without any professional or design background, or education for that matter:

"In some ways it was rougher, due to my lack of knowledge about the practical aspects of design. For example, the first thing I was asked to do in my new position was to build a 'mechanical' for my boss—I literally had no idea what a mechanical was and had to Google the word (which was an extremely fruitless endeavor given how many meanings that word has). Luckily, there was another designer here who took me under her wing, and showed me how to do these mechanicals, and all the other stuff I presume one is taught in design school: how to make a markup, spec colors, format type, etc. I badgered her with questions incessantly during the first week. But, the good news was that all of those design skills were easy enough to acquire some competence in. It's the design itself that's proven more difficult.

"Conversely, because I had no training, I also had no preconceptions about what a design career should be, and thus:

1) I wasn't disappointed by all the repetitive and menial labor it requires (not to mention humility), and

2) I wasn't over-awed by the design gods I was working with.

ROBERTO CALASSO

AUTHOR OF

The Marriage of Cadmus and Harmony

Peter Mendelsund: K (Knopf, 2004)

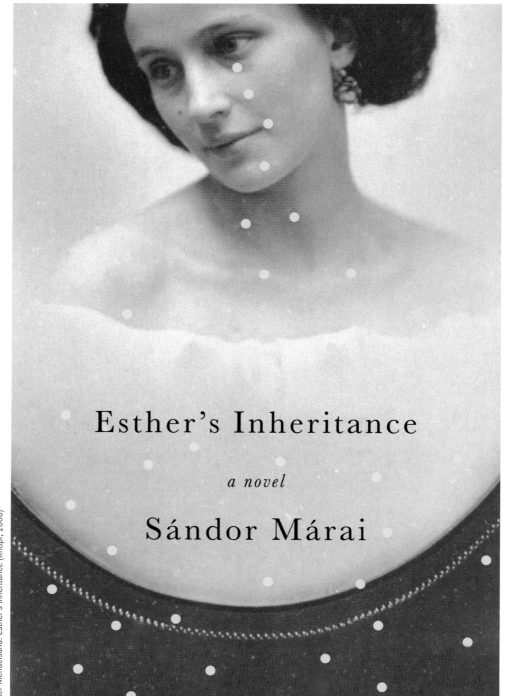

"I remember once, long ago, a designer told me how nervous she would be if she ever had the opportunity to meet Chip Kidd. Well, for me, knowing nothing about design, Chip was, and always has been, just my friend who happens to work next to me. So there were no nerves at all. It always seemed like just another job—a very fun job—but really just a job."

He's quite clear on the way things worked out for him and never regrets not having gone to a design school:

"My feeling has always been that I have learned more about design by looking around me carefully (observing life, collecting impressions of the visual culture all around) than I would have learned in academia. Designers should naturally be visual magpies—amassing images, storing them, thinking hard about why some are beautiful and some are not, assimilating these lessons and putting them to work. If you don't have that urge, maybe design is the wrong field for you. Keep a scrapbook, save the tuition money.

"I suppose that one makes contacts in school that prove helpful in the job hunt. And it's always useful to have someone with a good eye to help you prune your portfolio.

"The one mistake I made, I think, in preparing my portfolio was including too much in it. It would have been great to have someone say 'less!'. Now, would I need a whole semester-long portfolio class to figure that out? I hope not."

So there you have it: to go to school, or to not go to school. There is no question. All you have to do is absorb knowledge like a sponge, think, rethink, and think again. Read when you are not thinking and practice your design skills as much as possible.

Consider education a diving board into a pool, but do not give up swimming because the board is not your thing, really. One of the main characteristics of true creativity is curiosity for all things new and different.

WHICH WAY DO YOU PREFER WORKING?

Alone = 27.3%

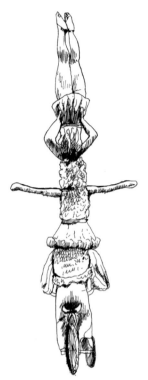

In a small team = 58.0%

In a big team = 1.1%

Paired up = 13.5%

WELCOME
TO WONDERLAND

Looking for work can be extremely frustrating, especially if you don't have any income at the time. This is when you need to do what most people hate the most—sell yourself. You need attend interviews, impress your prospective employers with a portfolio that tells the story of your work even if you're not there, and interact and show some personality. Here, we'll give you a few tips and assure you that soon enough it will all be over, including your nervousness.

Once you start—and every beginning is a bit tough—you will suddenly face a lot of unfamiliar, stressful situations. You're not in Kansas anymore and you can't allow yourself the same mistakes you could make in school because nobody could fire you. You're dealing with real clients, deadlines, and money, and the repercussions of a badly done job can be much greater. You'll probably start out working with someone or in a team, sharing responsibilities—in sickness and in health. But we actually like to think that this the fun part.

Roll Up Your Sleeves

The first step is always the most diffi-cult. It makes no difference whether you are looking for a nine-to-five gig in a big-league agency, whether you are hoping to work for a small studio where the hours are long but the cre-ative satisfaction is rewarding, or whether you are looking for a job for the first or the fifth time. The only place to start is at the beginning.

You need to consider the same param-eters that determined your choice of school:

Where do you want to work? If you think this is an easy question, think again. Every designer has his or her top three design jobs, but there are plenty of other studios where you can learn.

What do you want to specialize in? Do you have any special skills or experi-ences that might give you an advan-tage? Weigh what you can get and what you can offer, and keep it in mind when you contact future employers.

Where do you see yourself in one, three, or five years? Give it some thought, then draw up a plan. Not a rigid manifesto, but a loose timeline of your wishes that will allow you to grow and change your mind along the way.

The Hunt

Looking for work is the most stressful part of being a designer. You're never the only candidate, and competition is often stiff. It can be very frustrating and embarrassing trying to sell your-self when you know they know you don't know what you're worth.

You might bluff your way up, as did Like Ora Ito. The young Frenchman's path to fame and fortune was ingen-ious, if reckless. At twenty-one, Ito, whose real name is Ito Morabito, decided he couldn't bear spending ten years inching his way up the career lad-der. So, the son of well-known Paris fashion designer Pascal Morabito invented the pseudonym Ora Ito to carve out his own identity. Without using his father's money or connec-tions, he set out to excite the design world with an audacious media stunt. He helped pen two articles for the fashionable French magazines *Crash* and *Jalouse*, presenting a selection of 3D images of completely made-up products for such mega-brands as Louis Vuitton, Apple, and Levi Strauss & Co.

The response was electric. Within weeks of the first article's publication,

It's website was receiving 200,000 visitors a day. A Swiss collector and numerous wristwatch fans wanted to buy the designer's four imaginary Swatch designs, whose digital red dials and cool curves added a futuristic edge to the company's classic look, even though no such products existed. Customers inundated luxury goods company LVMH Moët Hennessy/Louis Vuitton with calls and store visits in a desperate attempt to buy Ito's proposed monogrammed backpack. A factory in China bestowed the ultimate accolade. It lifted the designs and started churning out counterfeits. "It was wild," recalls Ito, noting that no companies initiated legal action against him because the designs were virtual and well received by consumers.[8]

Bluffing can be quite risky though, and there are many other ways of creating a buzz around your work. Put it up on design blogs or send it to magazine editors or even throw an exhibition with some friends. Get out there. Strut your stuff.

But before impressing the world with your work you need two documents to achieve greatness: your resume and your portfolio.

Resume

This document is crucial. The difficult part about creating one is knowing what to include and what to highlight.

When writing your resume, have in mind that the people who will evaluate it have at least a dozen more to look through in that afternoon. So make it clear, short, and succinct. A handwritten description on a mess of colored papers complete with colorful collages of rainbows and unicorns is unacceptable from professional creative people. No, no, no.

Ideally your CV should not exceed one A4 page, and should clearly represent information about your life (age, place of birth/residence), education (stick to the important bits—no need to get into the details of the paper maché workshop you attended in high school), previous work experience (again, stick to the relevant—think about what will be interesting to the person/company that receives it), skills (if you have a good hand for drawing or an eye for photography, don't be shy to add them to the usual photoshop/illustrator skill set) and, finally, think about what extra skills you possess (speaking another language or two or having a degree in sociology might turn out to be your secret superpower).

If you have previous work experience and you're still talking to your ex-boss ask him to write you a letter of recommendation, which you should attach to your resume. This letter outlines briefly what position you held within the company as well as how satisfied they were with your performance and what you contributed to the team, the company, or to overall performance.

Portfolio

You are your first client. Make your portfolio look great. Make it attractive, bursting with genius that spans all the areas in which you are comfortable working.

Use it as a visual communication tool (of which you are supposed to be a master).

Today, portfolios come in two major formats—an online portfolio and a "classic" physical one filled with tangible examples of your work.

Online portfolios serve as baits. If you do not have a webpage or a blog showing your work and contact info, you are missing out big time. You do not have to know how to code advance ActionScript or know how to perfectly optimize web applications, update daily, or implement a fresh redesign every few months (unless you are a Web designer, of course).

Simple, out of the box, technical solutions work just as well. Just dedicate yourself to posting on the Web. There are people getting hired this very second because someone saw their layout on Flickr or because they were found randomly wherever people from your neck of the woods go to look for visual inspiration.

Your portfolio is a marketing tool intended to sell the most valued product you have—you. It is proof of your education and testament to your experience, talent, and ability to resolve visual communication problems. Hence, visual and verbal elements should be balanced and thought out, made functional and easy to open with accessible examples and samples. Do not make your interviewer sweat. Make the portfolio work for him.

Greig Anderson designed a mailer piece in order to reach out to the agencies in Sydney and try to get work:

"I spent a long time building a website to showcase my work online but I felt that it was important to produce something physical which was tactile and could be sent to individuals personally and become another piece of work in itself."

By designing a poster containing various project examples, he found a good way to show work at a reasonable size and quality whilst also creating something which would perhaps be used or put up on the wall and not end up in a drawer:

"It was important to me that each mailer, when sent, could be individually personalized for the recipient, so I created a design for a card sleeve which used the "this" of the mailer and added "is for you" and gave me an opportunity to print each recipients name and address without the need to stick on a separate label and ruin the overall look and feel."

Experienced designers claim the first eight to ten images sell the work, but you will not be judged on the images alone. Be prepared to describe the client, their brief, and how your design worked for them. This allows for a better sales pitch, showing your prospective client more than just an aesthetic quality, but also your ability to negotiate practical aspects of a project, too.

You've chosen to apply to a particular company for some reason—you like their work, you think you can grow there—and whatever the reason, now you will need to communicate this to your potential employer.

Greig Anderson
Graphic designer
Sydney, Australia
After graduating Greig has been working at the multidisciplinary agency Curious in Glasgow, Scotland. Under the name Effektive, he freelances and works on self-initiated projects including button badges, posters and T-shirt designs. Apart from that he's a contributor and writer on the design blog The Serif. Greig is about to head off to Sydney to gain further experience as a designer.
www.effektivedesign.co.uk

Greig Anderson (Effektive): Self-promotional CV/Mailer (self-initiated, 2008)

Greig Anderson (Effektive): Self-promotional CV/Mailer (self-initiated, 2008)

Customize your portfolio for each studio/agency, if you can. Ask yourself, what type of work does this agency or company do? What projects can I show that best illustrate how I would help their business? Remember, your prospective employer is looking at you as someone who would be working within their existing team, culture, and practices.

Which brings us to the importance of personal presentation. Most of the time, if you have been called in, clients are already familiar with your work, so what they are really interested in is you! They want to be able to evaluate your enthusiasm, intelligence, energy and passion, as well as your skills.

Explain what part you played in each project you present—did you do everything? If it was a website, did you build it as well as create the design? Did you go outside your area of specialty or were you responsible for a project end-to-end? This can be an important factor in their decision making.

Be able to tell a story about your work. Be honestly critical about it, as your ability to evaluate work objectively is to your advantage.

In the case that you have to drop off your portfolio and do not have a chance to narrate in person, label your work with very short descriptions.

Other people's work is more available than ever and browsing through various portfolios involves a risk of (un)intentionally following a certain style or look that is trendy at the time. Your portfolio should display your true values as a designer and apart from flashy personal projects it should contain examples of technical skill as well as commercial work as those are the ones most clients go for.

The Job Interview

Job interviews are tough but they do get easier once you've gone through a few. You should make a point of attending them even if you have already secured another job, as it is a valuable experience that will improve your presentation skills and show you what are interviewers are looking for from you.

If you do not get a job, be honest with yourself and examine why you didn't, and try to correct possible errors or improve your work to the level required. Maybe you just need to build your experience before moving on to your dream job?

Checklist before you go get 'em, tiger
Portfolio (digital and/or printed)
Interview skills
Letters of recommendation
Academics, grades or class rank

Some of the most-often mentioned qualities that interviewers are looking for are:
Motivation/passion
Commitment
Openness to new ideas and critiques
Ability to articulate your work
"Team-material"

After hiring around forty designers in the three studios he built, Mark Ury has quite a good idea about the qualities he wants in a designer:

"You look for curiosity, language skills, and craftsmanship. Those are the three that matter, and in that order. If they aren't curious, they won't discover things others can't see. If they can't verbalize what they've seen or their ideas on why it's important, they can't sell the solution. And if they don't have the craft skills, they can't deliver what they promised."

Apart from these things you need to learn how to interact with other people, whether they are your colleagues, clients, bosses, or employees. Make sure you demonstrate those skills in the interview.

Be polite but persistent and do some research before calling up your prospective employer, office, or agency. It's crucial to know the name of the person with whom you are hoping to get an interview, even if they are not hiring at the moment.

Once you establish contact, send your resume and arrange a meeting. Re-check the meeting schedule a day before, which serves as a reminder (yes, busy people forget) and a way to make sure it is still on.

Prior to the interview, organize some presentation materials that will show off your skill and ability to the interviewer. Create yourself a neat set of stationery, such as business cards and branded folders to hold your work. Business cards cost next to nothing, but they can get you places. Without them you will not even get freebies at trade shows. Extra effort put in your presentation materials will not go unnoticed. People have been employed simply for binding their portfolios into neat black little books instead of presenting dull CDs and normal pieces of paper.

Get Ready for Some Cross-Examining

As with any other job interviews, certain standard questions will be asked. They usually begin with something like "So, why are you here?" or "Tell me a little about yourself." Your answers should fit within given selection criteria and at the same time display your skills and know-how. Be sure to mention experiences (if you have any that are relevant to the position you are applying for). Explain why you want to work for this particular company, based on the research you have done and your long-term career goals. Be sincere. Which brings us to the scary part of the interview—"What kind of salary you expect?" Do not

STRUGGLE !!!

keep learning and working hard

determination

TALENT PASSION SKILL THE RIGHT PEOPLE TO WORK WITH!

keep as open mind and work harder than GOD

Doing your best & using your contacts

A Bit of everything. Just have great ideas and your set.

IMAGINATION

PASSION

to care more about having fun than money

Productivity and selling

ENJOYING WHAT YOU DO !!

finding the balance. and love.

The ability of think, question, and response.

Never stop using your fantasy and always try to be better than your last job.

HARD WORK

LUCKY

Being in the right place at the right time, networking, treating people well, and a bit of skill for good measure.

Drive as well as a hunger to learn.

COMPROMISING

4 things in order of importance : TALENT, MOTIVATION (to find meaning in what you do), Be aware of your enviroment, SELF-DISCIPLINE.

Having enough spare time for not being a designer...

Speed in some cases ... Quality in others... talent always (but it takes all kinds)

Selling, skill, productivity - you can have it without these three

OBSESSION

PERSISTANCE

Skills, self motivation and the ability to sell an idea to a client.

teamwork, teamwork and teamwork. Being tight as a team makes it fun to go to work

WORK HARD & BE NICE TO PEOPLE

love, determination, no sleep

being pro-active

ADAPTATION tru thru OBSERVATION

KNOWLEDGE

confidence and assertiveness

Good for promoting the design industry, but it's not something I like to participate in.

jump to answer. Take a deep breath, and return the question. What is the usual salary for this position? If you are lucky, you will draw that information out of your interviewer. If not, say it depends on the details of the job and give a wide range.

Even if you are not specifically asked, be sure to mention what else you're good at—problem-solving, organization, interpersonal communication, focusing on projects, specific expertise. If you lack experience be sure to mention that you are a "hard-working quick learner."

Quite often interviews end with "Do you have any questions for us?" so you had better prepare some. If your question makes sense it will impress the interviewer. Plan your questions the same way you will plan your answers, but do not ask about holidays or benefits. If they have made no mention of the salary, this might be a good time to initiate that conversation. Don't feel uncomfortable; you deserve to get paid for what you'll be doing.

Try to keep communication a two-way street, a dialogue, as this will help you and the interviewer decide if you are a good match for the position. At the end of the interview thank your interviewers for their time and the opportunity to talk to them. Once you leave the interview room, mull over the meeting for bit. Did you get any "off guard" questions or bungle some answers? Address these issues in preparation for the next interview.

Most interviewers will let you know when to expect an answer from them. If you are not contacted by that time, feel free to call them. If you have found a better position elsewhere by the time they express their interest, be sure to let other prospective employers know as soon as possible. Keep track of all your interviews as well as people to whom you've talked.

You got the job? Congratulations!

Modus Operandi

"Modus operandi" is just a ten-dollar Latin word for 'mode of operation,' that is, the way you work. Different models work for different people and types of organizations.

Depending on how big the studio or agency is, what purpose it serves and what services it performs, different rules apply. Some individuals work better in a strict environment with closer supervision, other work better in a flat hierarchy that offers more flexibility. It might take you a while to find out which model renders you happiest and most efficient.

Everyone works differently. Some sit in front of the computer and stare until they get focused enough; others skip between projects or tasks as one becomes boring or too complicated to tackle at the moment. The habits of one's production are not easily changed.

The question is, when you get a bunch of creative individuals in one room, how do you make them get along or even cooperate happily on projects that are not their primary interest (private projects lurking behind their glazed eyes, as you try to explain what, for whom, and where).

Some games cannot be played without a team. So how do you make a team? Perhaps you already started working during your studies, during which time you built a good network and gained enough experience and clients to begin a freelance practice right after graduation. Most people, however, begin their professional careers seeking employment in studios or agencies.

Working in a team makes you a better person, let alone a better designer. You learn to communicate and coexist with other people in a small space for lengths of time.

There is always someone to lean on when you are tortured by a client, someone whose opinion will help you out of a lurch, even someone to pick up a project where you left off. All-nighters seem less of a pain if there are friends and colleagues to share them.

Collaboration, discussion, and several heads (always better than one) working on the same project provide clients with extra thinking power and ideas, and ultimately strengthen your design team.

Julia Hoffmann
Creative director
New York
Julia is the creative director of advertising and graphic design at MoMA (Museum of Modern Art). She previously worked as an art director at the advertising agency Crispin Porter + Bogusky and Pentagram Design. Born in Frankfurt, Germany, Julia studied graphic design at the School of Visual Arts in New York, where she is now a member of the faculty.
www.juliahoffmann.com

Julia Hoffmann shared her working experiences with us:

"The best experiences working in a group have been during my time at Crispin Porter Bogusky. You always have a partner, and for brainstorming you need more than just yourself. The roles should be clearly defined though, because as soon as someone feels unnecessary, he'll slack off. So I love it when the group is diverse. When everyone has their own specialty, which nobody else has, that also makes it easy to divide the work and responsibilities."

There are people who achieve their best results working in teams; they get their best ideas in an open discussion with others and feel more comfortable when they work with friends.

On the other hand, this can end up being tricky, as you can really like someone on a personal level as well as the quality of their work, but if you don't share the same work ethics, your collaboration is unlikely to last, which can have a profound effect on your friendship.

Who is Who?

It is essential to know your responsibilities as well as those of others, and if you're starting in a place that employs more than three people the burden gets split between more people and each becomes a bigger expert in their field. The following job descriptions apply to positions in advertising agencies as well as larger studios.

The person most likely to interview you is the art director or creative director. The creative director is a department head responsible for the entire creative output. He or she approves and oversees almost everything produced. His or her right hand is the art director, whose duty it is to choose and handle outsourced production artists as well as designers on staff. This person is responsible for the final look and feel of the produced artwork. In

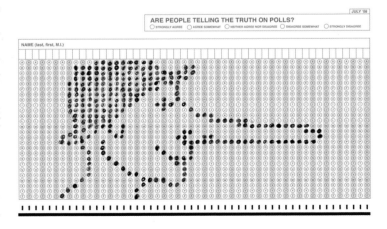

NUMBER OF MEN IN THE UNITED STATES WHO WILL DIE IN 2008 AS A RESULT OF...

CANCER (all types):

307,655

SKIN CANCER:
7,258

COLON CANCER:
21,289

PROSTATE CANCER:
26,987

BRAIN CANCER: SIX THOUSAND EIGHT HUNDRED AND TWELVE

LUNG CANCER: **96,835** | PANCREATIC CANCER: *16,785* | HEART DISEASE: **316,968**

HYPOTHERMIA: 449 | HEAT-STROKE: *207* | FIREWORKS ACCIDENT: 5 | FIRE: **1,737**

CAR ACCIDENT: **17,463**

FALLING FROM A CLIFF:
57

SHARK ATTACK:
ONE

LIGHTNING STRIKE:
40

FOREIGN OBJECT LEFT BEHIND DURING SURGERY:
2

ALCOHOL POISONING:
270

BEE, HORNET, OR WASP STING:
43 | FALLING DOWN STEPS: **1,062**

MOTORCYCLE ACCIDENT: **4,624**

COLLISION WITH OR BLOW FROM SPORTS EQUIPMENT: SEVEN

ELECTROCUTION: 374 | FALLING FROM A BUILDING: **504**

SUICIDE:
26,132 | LOU GEHRIG'S DISEASE: 3,420

ALZHEIMER'S DISEASE: 23,898 | BEING HIT BY A CAR: **3,920**

HOMICIDE:

STROKE: **55,105**

12372

THE FLU: 469

EARTHQUAKE, AVALANCHE, OR LANDSLIDE: TWENTY-EIGHT

DIVING INTO SHALLOW WATER: **47** | HIV/AIDS: **8,423**

SPIDER BITE: FIVE

Illustration by JULIA HOFFMANN *FOR MEN'S HEALTH MAGAZINE*
Numbers are projected estimates based on mortality figures from the Centers for Disease Control and Prevention WONDER database and the FARS Encyclopedia.

Julia Hoffmann: The Odds of Men Dying (*Men's Health*, 2007)

some cases, an art director does a large part of the creative director's work, so some companies choose not to have both "D"s on their payroll.

Senior designers do less design work and are more involved with decision-making. If they are lucky, they have several junior designers to do all the actual permutations and the dirty work, as seniors are concerned with overall concepts and the visual coherence of the material produced. In some cases, seniors are solely involved in coming up with ideas, which the juniors must manifest.

Junior designers are newbies in advertising agencies' or studios' creative departments who have just begun to learn the tricks of their trade. They do what they are told and work on a variety of projects from books and magazines to corporate identities, film titling, and multimedia interfaces.

In advertising agencies, designers often work closely with copywriters; they develop strategies and design concepts, write, edit, and proof promotional texts for a whole spectrum of media. If copywriters specialize in development of content for websites, they are often referred to as content developers and work closely with Web designers.

Web designers have to handle a host of rules and work in different teams. Their work starts with interfaces, site navigation, and visual execution, creating static or dynamic pages. Programmers then add functionality by creating Web applications and databases, all of which are supervised by a Web producer.

Once the artwork is completed and ready for print, the first person to handle it is a print production artist, who produces final files according to printer specifications, ensuring the artwork comes out of the printer with the proper appearance. In smaller agencies and companies, designers have to do their own pre-press and supervise the print production, so being versed in this knowledge is a big bonus.

Within the agencies, all work is divided between the creative and the client service department. Strategic planners and account managers perform the function of messengers between these two worlds. There are infinite variations on these titles, but, mainly, their duties are as follows.

The strategic planner needs to know the client's needs and wants, so he can relate that to consumer demand. He helps create single-minded creative briefs, which are very important for the further development of advertising campaigns.

Account managers handle client accounts, arrange deadlines in cooperation with creative departments, try to keep production within budget, and bring cold business reasoning to the oft-flamboyant creativity of the designers. Their main weapons are good briefs and meeting reports.

In-house designers, working in the art departments of various companies, are often shunned and neglected by many designers as it does not fit into the "cool" hype surrounding designers today. An in-house designer is more likely to have predictable hours, paid benefits and a healthy workflow pace. Some consider such positions a comfortable, stable option with consistent career development.

Sometimes in-house designing can be a thankless job and one often lacking in creative projects. Such designers are excluded from the creation of the marketing strategies they must later implement. On the other hand, these designers' understanding of the brand for which they are working can make or break the company's reputation. However you see it, this is a more comfortable option to the agency burnout process.

Playing in a team requires you to be aware of your place. Division of labor only works if every person does their part.

Our definitions of roles are to be taken with a pinch of salt, as their borders tend to blur. Besides, creative professions typically have a more organic structure/hierarchy, and the title you get on your business card is not always the most reliable description of your actual job.

Julia Hoffmann has changed quite a few business cards in her time:

"First I was hired as senior interactive designer to work on websites (although I never designed websites before). Quickly I realized that in advertising they treat designers as people who execute ideas, and I enjoyed working on the other side, to actually come up with the ideas, so they promoted me to an art director position a few months later. I started working with a partner on pitches that not only involved interactive media, but also traditional media. After six months they made me a design director for the Volkswagen account.

Gui Borchert
Art director
New York

Gui began his career as a graphic designer in Rio de Janeiro, Brazil, after which he moved to New York to work for R/GA in interactive advertising. He joined Mother New York in July 2007 to pursue new challenges in integrated advertising. Gui's strengths include idea generation and conceptual work, as well as design direction and execution. His diverse style can be seen across the variety of his work.

www.guiborchert.com

Gui Borchert:
Cover (*Sign Cafe* magazine, 2008)
Design by Nature (Nike Free, 2005)

"Although I had three different job descriptions, it's a place where you do everything all the time anyway so titles didn't really matter."

Do not think art directors have all the fun coming up with the ideas while you have to do the dirty work. Instead, focus on learning from them and letting them guide you. Your work can be fun and interesting even if it's dirty.

Gui Borchert is an art director at Mother New York, and he's still very much involved in the actual design process and loves it:

"I strongly believe that the closer you are to the work, the better (and more fun!). I also believe that great art directors should be great designers as well, and that is what I strive for every day. I hope that even decades from now, no matter how senior I may be, I am still very close to the work, and getting my hands dirty. Because that is what I really love about creative work—the actual process of figuring out what needs to be communicated, then creating a concept around an awesome idea for it and finally executing it in the best possible way, closely involved every step of the way."

YES NO
WRONG RIGHT
BIG SMALL
CASH ART
LOVE SEX
LAUGH CRY
LESS MORE
BLUE RED
FULL EMPTY
EVIL SAINT
ACTIVE PASSIVE
NOTHING EVERYTHING
WAR PEACE
COME GO
LOUD QUIET
ALWAYS NEVER
LATER NOW
NICE ASSHOLE
HERE THERE
HELLO GOODBYE
ASLEEP AWAKE
HEAVEN HELL
STUPID SMART
EVERYWHERE NOWHERE
CRAZY NORMAL
GOOD BAD
CLEAN DIRTY
HEALTHY SICK
FORGIVE REVENGE
DO DON'T
WORST BEST
NO YES

GOOD.

Gui Borchert: Conflict (LVHRD poster competition, 2007)

The most valuable advice he wants to pass along is:

"Always work with people you can learn from, that you respect, and that respect you back. Be passionate, work hard, do what you love. And never let anyone make you feel like you aren't good at what you do—but when it happens, use it to your advantage and just work harder to get even better at what you do. It works every time."

Practicing Patience

One of the most difficult tasks for every designer is learning how to evaluate and calculate time needed for a certain project. On average, spending more time on a project necessarily produces better results, but sometimes problems are solved in a moment of instant-genius.

Julia Hoffmann told us about her working marathons:

"It was the true test of how long can you really stay up and still make sense. My record was 52 hours with not even a nap. But working there cannot be counted in hours, more like in ideas. So 100 hours a week maybe sounds like a lot, but it's not, if you consider nobody forces you to work that much and you are having fun."

Every start is rough and you might feel like an idiot on more than a few occasions doing boring, uncreative, repetitive, or whichever other kind of task you weren't hoping for when you applied for the job.

If you identify yourself in this situation, keep in mind that working your way up to more creative freedom and nicer projects is proportionate to the time and effort invested in previous ones. Being on time, being a good workmate and not complaining will earn you the respect of your colleagues as well as superiors. Being an eager beaver and doing overtime just to run that extra mile will earn a lot of points for you, but be careful about ending up exploited.

Teamwork

Having other people involved in your work means learning how to be a team player. (Un)fortunately, your interpersonal skills rarely shine in their full glory during a job interview. That is why you get to use them later on. And you will use them a lot.

Working in a team will challenge your ways of thinking and lead to better results in the end. If you feel you cannot contribute much, this feeling will pass the first time you and your teammates accomplish something together. Not being alone on a job means sharing the good and the bad, the workloads, the ideas, and the concepts. It can be difficult to get used to, but is rewarding in the end.

To keep your team functioning like a big happy family, each member should equally value the others.

Respect not only comes from how good or important someone's work on the team is, but also from how good a person and a colleague he or she is.

There will be trouble, but all good team players must engage in dialogue. If you are capable of understanding the modus operandi of your workmates and finding a middle ground, conflicts can eventually be resolved.

Not all conflicts will be resolved through a calm exchange of opinions. Sometimes egos will clash, resulting in confrontation and anger.

This cannot be avoided, unless you work alone, or make an extra effort to avoid arguments.

Conflicts arise especially during long and tiresome projects, when people get most tense and are most likely to articulate their anguish. Sometimes reasons are even less obvious, but it is important to identify the real source of the conflict to be able to resolve it quickly and without bias. Sometimes company policies cause conflicts among employers, but you should transfer those problems to the company management and get on with your life.

Taking initiative in resolving problems doesn't mean everyone else will think you're pushy or trying to take over.
Do not permit bad language or water-cooler gossip, as it poisons the "water" for all team members. Ban backstabbing. Group leaders should be authoritative and resolve or mediate conflicts, enabling everyone return to "normal" as soon as possible.

Mark Ury
Experience architect
Toronto, Canada
Mark is an experience architect and occasional
entrepreneur. When he's not busy fussing with
business, he fusses with ideas, particularly
those at the intersection of products, services,
technology, and culture. Mark is currently chief
experience architect at Blast Radius. He is part
service designer, brand consultant, business
strategist, and geek.
www.blastradius.com

Chief architect and ECD: Mark
Ury/designer: Mauricio Pommella/Blast
Radius: dingo (Intrawest, 2006)

Even though to some people it comes more natural to lead (and most don't seek to be leaders at all), the ones who are keen on it can develop certain abilities, and even learn different "styles" of leadership.

One Leader to Rule Them All?

To paraphrase Mark Ury, a good leader makes a good team:

"A good leader sets the vision, picks the right team members, distributes the load between the players and the stars, fires the underperformers, and searches everywhere for the best talent. A good leader avoids toxic clients, shuts down projects that are hurting the team, pushes for regular hours and good pay, and takes the heat when things go bad. A good leader does all of this but then turns around to the team and demands they to do their best work. That's the deal: I passed you the ball—run with it."

"Good leaders inspire people, bring out the best in them and tame the shrew so all can work and play together. They are figures of authority, which sometimes makes them less popular, but they should be concerned more with being fair and efficient anyway.

"The primary duty of any good leader would be to build confidence in people around them by recognizing their achievements, as most people want to feel appreciated and valued. They need to have confidence in their subordinates as well, delegating some of the authority without letting go of supervision and control.

"Leaders need to make designers feel prepared to meet any challenge, through constant updates and growth of their knowledge and skills, and by making them feel confident in their abilities. Be their coach. Show them what good performance looks like using concrete examples of good presentations, reports, or client meetings. Give them useful feedback that is helpful and productive, not vague and judgmental. Show them how to improve through suggestions and solid reasoning derived from their work.

"As you build people's skills and confidence they become more and more willing to tackle larger challenges, which makes you an example of a good leader. Be someone who sets high standards and challenges people to do more, to think and act outside the box."

The entire experience orchestrated...

down to the
smallest detail

Chief architect and ECD: Mark Ury/designer: Mauricio Pommella/Blast Radius: dingo website layout, structure and moodboard (Intrawest, 2006)

Mario Hugo
Freelance
New York
Mario Hugo is a New York-based artist and designer. Though he spends an inordinate amount of time in front of his computer, Mario still feels most honest with a pencil and two or more sheets of paper. His first nine-to-five studio job was his last; he doesn't like the structure and tedium of a traditional office so he just dove into freelancing.
www.loveworn.com

Instead of telling people exactly how to do things, try telling them what to do and have them surprise you with their results.

Freelancing

If you feel you are not cut out for this kind of work, maybe you were born to be a freelancer. Freelancers are the lone wolfs, the mavericks, the free spirits. They cannot play for the team, as they prefer to work on their own. They often get sucked into teams of companies or studios for which they work, but they keep to themselves.

Being surrounded by a lot of people can be burdensome, but there is no doubt it can also motivate you and create a more stimulating environment. A freelancer without self-discipline is a dead freelancer. However, they tend to be a bit more "free" when they are off the leash, to say the least.

There is nothing Mario Hugo prefers more than creating artwork under his own terms and in his underwear:

"I think I thrive with a little chaos. I love making pictures, and I work well under pressure. I may complain, but I [usually] enjoy looming deadlines and quick turnaround times—visceral, gut solutions are sometimes the best, and

projects don't occupy me too much for too long. It's important that my clients and projects run the creative gamut. Too much of any one thing is definitely boring and it's harder to stay disciplined."

Creative disorder sometimes can take its toll, especially when it comes to organizing your working time. Burning both ends of the candle is dangerous, but you are also free to kick back and do nothing after a working spell. Work hard, but do not forget to play equally hard.

"My schedule is very amorphous—I think it makes my process more organic and interesting, but it can be troublesome at times. I may work fourteen days in a row with 3 a.m. nights, but sometimes I'll dismiss projects and take two weeks for vacation. It evens out, and I try not to draw big distinctions between personal work and client work, so I'd say I'm very frequently working, but not always for client ends."

One of the disadvantages of freelance work is its unpredictability. You never know how much work will you have next week. Of course, if you are good and work hard on self-promotion, you should be all right.

Mario Hugo: A Fanciful William Morris (Cavalier exhibition, 2006)

Mario Hugo: Flaunt 83 (Flaunt, 2007)

"Freelancing is like that old adage—feast or famine. I may not have had a job for a couple weeks, but when Santa calls or writes about a new project, I can bet a couple elves and the tooth fairy are going to have projects for me later that day. Perhaps something cosmic is at play—I can't prove it, but it's absolutely incredible how many projects land all at once! Unfortunately, I have to turn a couple projects down when I was totally free those previous two weeks—this is a big drawback. There are times when I worry a bit—but that risk is also a bit exciting, and I take that time to focus on other personal projects, exhibitions, etc."

Freelancers feel imprisoned in an ordinary office. It is the peer pressure of belonging to an organized structure and imposed rules that make them freak out. This "prison" feeling they get while being employed by somebody else is hard to explain.

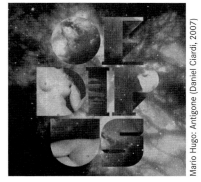

Mario Hugo: Antigone (Daniel Ciardi, 2007)

"My first nine-to-five studio job was my last, and I stayed there one year to the day. I'm not terribly pragmatic. Design and art are passions—they are more than occupations. I felt suffocated by an agency career, and I knew I'd never feel comfortable within those four walls. I don't like the structure and tedium of a traditional office—we freelancers tend to have eclectic tastes, interests, and goals. I just quit and dove into freelance, and that desperation really inspired me to experiment and grow as an artist. Now I work in my underwear."

YOUR DREAM CLIENT...   A CLIENT'S DREAM DESIGNER...

Lets you do whatever you want = 60.1%   Does exactly what the client wants = 37.5%

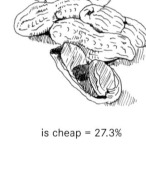

is famous = 9.1%   is cheap = 27.3%

is rich = 6.7%   is famous = 6.8%

DOWN THE RABBIT HOLE

For each and every one of us, freedom means a different thing. To some it means flexible working hours, to others infinite creative freedom or making your own rules and money; together they are a part of every designer's dream.

It's simple to become autonomous, as designers can work with a minimum of resources, creating miracles with only a pen, paper, and laptop. On the other hand, being your own boss brings a lot of other responsibilities, forcing you to spend more time being your own manager and accountant than actually designing stuff.

If you have already arrived at the point where you choose your clients, you probably already know how it feels to wish you weren't the one who has to pick up the phone.

It's time for you to learn things you might hate doing, while of course keeping a positive attitude, as you will need a lot of happy thoughts to be able to free-fall into independence.

Self-Employment It Is!

Thomas Ulrik
Designer and studio owner
London
T.U/studio is an independent multidisciplinary design project set up in London in 2007. Thomas works in the intersections between creative direction, identities, conceptual and considered communication, and typography. His clients run across a wide range of backgrounds from larger corporate and cultural institutions to magazines.
www.thomasulrik.com

he reasons for starting your own thing may be various in nature; maybe you're not happy with your present job because the money is bad or your ideas are ignored; perhaps you want to do what you want to do and when you want to do it, determining your own hours, taking time off when you feel like it, being in control of what direction you head, deciding which clients to work with, and handpicking your colleagues.

Many employees of design studios stay working for them only until they have a sufficient clientele of their own to start their studios. In those cases self-employment seems like a natural progression from a full-time job, even though in the beginning you will have to keep your day job and drag a lot of freelance work on the side.

Thomas Ulrik thinks one of the main reasons a lot of designers set up their own studio stems from a desire for autonomy in one's work:

"For me, at least, this was one of the main reasons for turning full-time independent.

I had worked at both large and small studios in the past, but it wasn't particularly a decision based on growing tired of this setup, but more of an organic process. I had recently moved to London from Copenhagen, and there was, at some point, an opportunity to setup alone due to a few projects that presented themselves—and I just acted on the basis of that."

He distinguishes among people who set up solo for purely instinctive and personal reasons and those that do so from a long-term plan of becoming a real company, with actual strategies for growth, and business plans:

Thomas Ulrik: The Vision Magazine (CPH Vision Fashion Fair, 2007)

"I think it was always in the back of my mind to start a studio, but the experience and tools that you get from working with large design consultancies is something I would never have wished to have been without.

"In London, you see so many people setting up alone straight out of art college, which is, in a way, completely refreshing and inspiring, but in some ways also seems a little limiting, because there is so much to be gained from other people who have been working with the crafts or the underlying politics behind larger design setups for a long time."

There are not many people who are mature enough to switch to freelance work or start their own studio straight from school. Getting a bit of experience someplace else might prove valuable, as you get to see how things work from the inside. Instead of figuring all those work modes out on your own and making your own errors and assumptions, just learn from the older and wiser.

If all this experience does not help in any other way, it will, at the least, allow you to appreciate the liberties of running your own show.

Beware of the Pitfalls

Freelancing or owning a studio can be hell—no steady income, uncertainty of work, none of the benefits, and a lot of overtime can turn you into a high-strung wire. The competition is overwhelming in numbers and abilities. While you waste time on contracts, legal issues, accounting, marketing, and other business functions or fork out money for professional services, *they* are focused on their work.

If you want to deliver quality, your work can take over your life. Be careful not to take on too much. Overload means loss of sleep and nerves as well your creative edge. And if this happens too many times, your clients will not be happy. Before accepting any jobs, consider the time you can afford a certain project and whether you can pull it off in a satisfactory manner. If you get a lot more work than you can handle, consider hiring help or outsourcing.

Even if you learn not to overload, you will work many evenings and weekends meeting deadlines. The worst part is the pressure of responsibility, as all of it is down to you and you only.

It can be very frustrating, working alone, coming up with all the ideas and making all the decisions yourself. Adding a few more people to your projects might bring a freshness to your work and make it a less lonely ride.

Thomas Ulrik always tries to have a completely open and constructive attitude toward the people he works with and their input:

"Most projects are run with frequent interaction with a client or other people. I rarely work in a way where ideas and images are developed completely isolated. This engagement of all parties involved, I think, leads often to a result where I will not be the only one that can claim ownership of the solution.

"The studio, technically, only constitutes of myself. It is built around an idea of loose associations, meaning that wherever possible I will work with other people in a collaborative manner. Although the freedom you get from working alone is good in some respects, I believe that the best work usually happens in the crossing and glitches between my own ideas and those of someone else.

"Collaborations don't necessarily have to happen in a designer/designer setting. Often the most inspiring people to work with, and thereby often wielding the best results, will be persons from completely different backgrounds.

"Designers tend to think—however 'creative' they might be—along much the same lines, and it is interesting where a project might end when working with someone coming from a more theoretically rooted background."

Something you cannot avoid in the beginning is undercharging. Work out your expenses and costs, then add 30 percent on top for all the other costs and you are probably still under the mark.

The process of setting your price requires confidence; remember that you are very good at your job, which is exactly why they want to hire you and not somebody else. Maybe you will give in to temptation in the beginning, lowering your prices and building up your client list, but the lower you go, the more overloaded you will get, initiating a vicious circle.

Another overload risk lies in failing to balance between projects that feed your belly and the ones that feed your brain/heart. Thomas often takes on projects to "pay the bills" as a deliberate strategy in order to then work on other things that are perhaps closer to the heart:

"Financially the studio functions very much hand-to-mouth. This is often a very conscious result, coming from the compulsive taking on of projects that don't pay anything alongside the ones that do. I am still in a personal situation where this is something I can get away with, as there are no kids or things of that matter yet.

"Some like the romantic version—that they never take on work because of the money.

"Money is often a breaking point when discussing a designer's attitude toward their practice, but to be honest this is not something that fills too much of my time. It's important, of course, to be attributed the due success a given project might have, which will often be financially.

"But there is no grand master plan for this. At times there is a more than a healthy financial aspect—and that's great. Other times there isn't, but then it will most likely come next time."

Remember, you need to come up with enough money every month to cover office rent, wages for accountants, collaborators or whichever kind of help you might be hiring, and general overhead. Sure, you can always come out on top by putting in a few extra hours, but look after yourself—you won't be getting any younger, and you won't be able to pull so many all-nighters in a row. Health is one of those things money can't buy.

Being on top of a chain of command is liberating, but being the only man behind the helm of a vessel in a daily working storm can get pretty hairy. It's a lot to handle, and you might feel the need to breathe into a paper bag more often than usual.

Overcoming this fear is essential. What's the worst thing that can happen? You'll have to find a job, but at least you've tried making it on your own.

Setting up

Financially and psychologically, the easiest way to start up a studio is by teaming up with one or more people with whom you already have a working relationship. This means becoming equals—that is, sharing the workload and owning equal parts of the company. You get to make the same decisions without being solely responsible, which takes off a lot of pressure.

People often team up either with someone who complements their talents (for example, your partner is better at Web and video, while your strengths are print and handling clients), or someone with whom they are in sync (for example, a designer with a similar style or compatible working methods), but in the end it's about finding people you trust and with whom you share ideas and work ethics.

In small groups, people connect faster but there is also the downside of hardly ever getting a break from one another. For Michael Lugmayr the key is in being open and honest:

"We talk, talk, talk... express feelings, express frustrations—that's what a 'good' team needs to keep going."

Toko
Graphic design studio
Sydney, Australia
Toko Graphic Design is a multidisciplinary design studio with the emphasis on print and environmental design. Established in Rotterdam, The Netherlands, in 2001, and now based in Sydney Australia, where it relocated in the beginning of 2006 to pursue new (geo)graphic adventures. Toko is heavily influenced by the rich Dutch traditions in art and design.
www.toko.nu

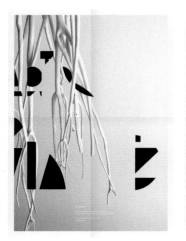

Michael Lugmayr/Toko: Photo Exhibition Collateral (Gallery Blik, 2004)

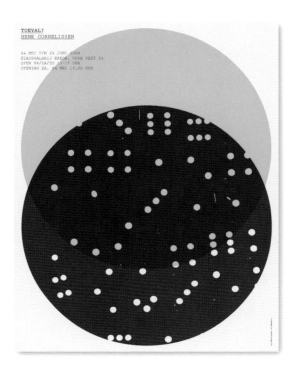

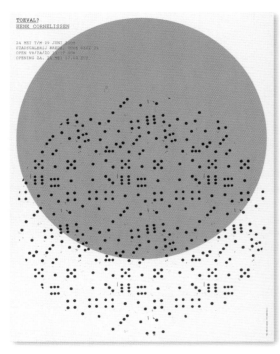

Eva Dijkstra, Michael Lugmayr/Toko: Toeval Design (Festival Breda, 2008)

Toko is a small studio in Sydney, Australia that consists of Michael Lugmayr, Eva Dijkstra, and a few interns. They evolved probably very much like any other enthusiastic designer that decided to start their own business—full of energy and ready to take on the world:

"We worked toward designing projects we really liked, both cultural and corporate. It was a natural transition. We did not set massive goals to push ourselves. We only decided to stay small as a studio to ensure quality and personality.

"Now six or so years ahead we are still ready to take on the world."

They divided all the responsibilities, both design and nondesign, between the two of them, but as business grows it's harder to do everything on your own:

"Except for the accountant we hired, we manage to do everything ourselves... having said that, in some circumstances it probably would have been better to outsource the one or the other.

"I guess it's all about being in the zone. Once you're used to doing it all, you will manage it somehow... Currently it's hardly possible to do it all so we will rethink the way we operate."

They found their size, now they need to fine-tune it:

"The best thing about keeping a studio small is having 'studio' personality and a clear overview of what will be delivered at the end of the day.

"We like to process projects in a sudden way and by being a small office we, 'sort of,' can control this, which is much harder for bigger firms. Our overhead is relative, which enables us to be pickier in taking on sudden projects, which is very different when you have twenty people to take care of."

As a downside to keeping it small they say there are not enough hours in a day.

Once you decide to start your own business be prepared for rough times as well as good times. Be prepared to work harder than ever before, but only to be able to smile, as it is all your own doing. Your business will go through thick and thin, so do not start it if you don't plan to have a positive outlook, even during the roughest times.

What Is a Design Studio?

The first (fun) task you will face as the proprietor of your own business is naming it. Naming your baby is a completely personal matter, so we'll stay out of that one, but we will remind you that some kids suffer more in school—and life in general—with names like Heaven or Chardonnay, bequeathed by parents who never thought twice about how this might influence their childhood.

Think of five words to describe your baby, and keep them as a guideline at all times.

A business plan is essential to organizing yourself. It is exactly what it says on the cover—a document that will outline your actions, allocate resources, and focus on key points and opportunities of your endeavor.

Banks and other funding bodies ask for a business plan with your applications for financing. As an official document, it needs to be well written and concise. It should contain a description of your company and its activities. There is no need for your business plan to be long, but it has to be sharp and clear since this is the essential idea you'll be communicating to the people with whom, or for whom, you work.

When writing your business plan make sure to include your company description, explaining how and when the company was formed, followed by a description of what are you selling.

Market analysis will show you know your market and that there is a need for your product. For the investors, you will have to outline a clear plan of attack, strategy and implementation.

Be specific, as this will earn you points with investors. Round it all up with a brief presentation of your management team and, of course, lots of Excel tables showing your financial plan. Include profit and loss accounts, a cash-flow breakdown and a balance sheet. When all this is good and ready, write an executive summary and use this as your cover page. Off course, divide the information into neat, presentable chapters.

Your plan is allowed to change over the course of time, depending on the development of your situation and your experience. Perhaps one part of your business is not proceeding according to plan due to stiffer-than-expected competition, or perhaps you have figured out ways to cut costs in a certain production stage because you have purchased machinery instead of outsourcing it. This may change the scope of your business altogether and maybe that of your company. Depending on where your company is registered, there might be benefits involved. Inform yourself properly about these kinds of opportunities.

The type of business you choose to register will determine what kind of work you are allowed to take on, as well as which tax rates will apply. Depending on your country of business and the tax system, certain types have advantages over others, which is why you should seek the advice of an accountant. Find a good one. The price is worth the ability of an accountant to increase your company's earnings and give you valuable advice. An accountant will ensure your books are in order and that your taxes are paid or deducted through equipment, rent, phone, or other office expenses.

Find yourself a bank manager, preferably a specialist in small businesses or a financial advisor. Some countries have government funds dedicated to assisting new business development.

We advise you always to sign a contract with all your clients, even if they are friends. The contract should define

timelines, the budget, and span of work. A retainer of 30 percent should be secured at that time in order to maintain your cash flow. An additional 30 percent should be received during the project and the remaining 40 percent upon completion. These figures, of course, depend on the scale of the project and the type of agreement you have with your client.

If work for a specific client is extensive, implement a bi-weekly or bi-monthly fee, so even if other clients are late with their payment or the job takes longer than expected you will have some money for bare necessities.

Cash flow is the balance of funds being received and paid through your companies account. It is the difference between money coming into a business from selling its products and the money it spends on all aspects of production. Keeping your cash flow as a positive value is vitally important in the smooth running, survival, and success of a business, so in the beginning you should revise it monthly.

A good customer base is essential. For a smoother transition from employed to self-employed, try building one out of your freelance jobs or from contacts during previous employment.

Getting New Work

Your ability to survive as a designer will be largely based on your ability to find new work and expand your client base, as you cannot depend on the few freelance projects with which you began. Getting clients to recommend your services to others requires a whole new set of skills and responsibilities. You need to be reliable and on time and able to create good work. As a rule, great work creates new work. Be sure to bring relevant and clear work to your presentations, and include it in your portfolio, as that is what most clients are looking for.

Scott Buschkuhl from Hinterland explained how this worked for his young studio:

"We haven't been in the industry long enough to say all assigned work comes from clients specifically seeking Hinterland out for work it has created for other companies: 50 percent of the work comes from referrals, 25 percent comes from clients seeing work we created for others in the past and 25 percent comes from us seeking out new business."

"Having your portfolio online isn't enough. Sometimes you need to dig deeper, look for more, and work on your relationship with your client.

"Hinterland's recipe for seeking out new business is made up of cold calling, email correspondence, and promotional materials sent out by mail. A wonderful trend I have noticed during the short existence of the studio is repeat business. I might do work for Client A, spearheaded by a specific person. That person then leaves Client A to work for Client B and contacts us again to help them develop another project. The great benefit to a working relationship such as this is that with each new project our shared past will influence and help evolve how we work together. The initial growing pains of a project no longer exist."

Creating great work is not one-sided. A lot of elements need to fall into place, from the client side to the studio, as Scott outlines:

"I think all clients will approach Hinterland with an idea of what they are looking for even in loose form, be it as simple as 'we are looking for a brochure for a specific event or an identity for our small startup.' Yet, the more restrictions imposed upon the studio, the more excited I become. Restrictions create challenges and challenges create an atmosphere for problem solving. I think the best possibilities for an outcome are achieved when each enters the process with a very open mind.

"I do not believe clients approach Hinterland for a specific 'style.' The studio's main goal is not to generate work that can fall under a specific 'house style' but to consistently produce quality idea-driven designs. As I often collaborate with a small group of other creatives, with a range of design sensibilities, the directions explored are unconfined to specific 'styles'. If Hinterland can collaborate with creators of quality photography/illustration, engaging writing and a good printer who understands a variety of creative possibilities or is willing to experiment then all the key elements are in place to create a successful project."

Who Do I Want for a Client?

Working for a client is a lot like being a psychologist or seducing a person. You have to know what they like and deal with every person's nuances and personalities. Charming them at meetings, calling them every day, and discussing problems with them amounts to getting paid for it all.

Schools rarely mention clients. They do not show you how to treat ideas and demands coming from a client, which is often very discouraging for new designers, who lose confidence in their work and start second-guessing their skills. Simulations of commissioned projects are like learning to ride a bike with training wheels. Once they are gone, it is so much easier to fall and scrape your artsy knees.

Scott Buschkuhl
Creative director and owner of Hinterland
New York
Founded in 2003 by Scott Buschkuhl and based in Brooklyn, Hinterland is a multidisciplinary design studio creating books, magazines, illustrations, packaging, identities, and more. They believe the best design comes from a close collaboration between studio and client, and work toward developing a solution that is engaging and effective.
www.hinterlandstudio.com

Hinterland: Before&After Promotional Brochure/Poster (self-initiated, 2008)

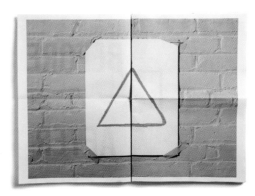

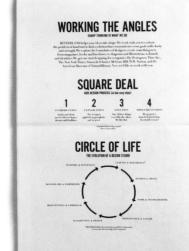

Hinterland: Before&After Promotional Brochure/Poster (self-initiated, 2008)

When working in the real world you should expect pain, tears, and maybe some blood, but get back on that bike if you want to ride alongside the big boys.

Work would be easy if it all went according to plan. Naturally, all of us plan to work for ideal, liberal, and utopian clients who always understand our ideas. Unfortunately, such clients are the roommates of Santa and the Easter Bunny, which makes them fictional characters who pay with virtual money. Fortunately, your fees can balance the effort and time spent on a project. So, instead of waiting for that ideal project that was tailored to you, make some choices on the client front. Namely, you will need to navigate between the two archetypal clients: difficult ones with challenging projects and easygoing ones that give you free reign on their boring projects.

Scott Buschkuhl explains how he copes with different sorts of clients and projects:

"There are three very simple studio-client relationships each project can fall under: Good Work/Bad Pay, Bad Work/Good Pay, and Good Work/Good Pay. Many people might think that the Good Work / Good Pay scenario would be ideal but that does not

always ring true. My feeling is that any studio that wants to succeed as a business will have to at some point entertain each and any of these scenarios. The variety of challenges from a difficult, easygoing, profitable and/or unprofitable client can all be the same. Even if Hinterland takes a project purely for profit to cover overhead, costs of a studio space, employees, etc, I will still get excited because I see Hinterland as a problem solver. No matter the restrictions we have to deal with, I try to keep the storytelling concise and brief, letting the end user get from point A to point B with ease. This is a formula I try to emulate with each and every project no matter if the client is difficult or giving."

Big or Small?

The bigger the client, the smaller you look in their office, the shorter the deadlines, and the more corrections you will get. Just kidding. Big brands usually have very rigid sets of brand rules compiled in a master tome called the brand book or brand manual, which you will need to take into consideration.

Always ask for this book in your initial meeting. If the client does not have one, consider suggesting creating one for the company.

Xavier Encinas
Art director and founder of peter&wendy
Paris
A graphic design studio based in Paris,
Peter&Wendy are living each project as a unique
process and experience while maintaining a
close relationship with their clients. A variety of
graphic projects is being produced: print, publishing, exhibition and event identity, corporate
identity and anything else that gets them excited enough to be involved.
www.peter-wendy.com

Large companies usually have several instances of decision making, which means you will wait several days for a verdict, even though corrections will need to be executed swiftly. Do not lose your nerves. Be polite and explain how much time you need to do the job properly. All large companies think they are your only client.

Low-key clients do not necessarily mean less effort. If you are any good, you have the power to rock their world. Only you can turn their invisible product into something new, palpable, and appealing to potential customers. You can make their record

Xavier Encinas/peter&wendy: Grotesque (self-initiated, 2008)

covers interesting even if their music is not. The smallest client in the world can be the highlight of your portfolio and good training for the big-time ones, who are sure to come if you are good and passionate about your work.

Give every project you work on your best shot and soon you will have twenty masterpieces with which to impress your competition and woo future clients.

Why waste time on self-promotional pieces when you can get paid for making great stuff for someone who really needs your professional help? No client is too small. Think like that and, eventually, you will score the kind of client everybody ultimately wants.

Xavier Encinas prefers to stay away from the big leagues:

"The good thing about working with small clients is that there are fewer people in the chain of command. So the projects are more easygoing.

"On the other side, sometimes there is less creativity because of less budget involved. Our projects always come with a strong production side, so when a client wants something really stunning and different, but he doesn't have enough money to produce it, it becomes tricky."

Xavier Encinas/peter&wendy: Bedeutung Magazine issue 1 (*Bedeutung Magazine*, 2008)

Communicate With Your Client

Being selective about who you work for and what you do for them is quite difficult when you're starting out and don't know when the phone is going to ring next. But saying no at certain times will keep you young, your work fresh, and will make the odds of you getting bored from the industry lower, as well as the ones for you burning out in the process.

That's exactly what kept Peter& Wendy in Neverland:

"We decided to take only the projects we really want to work on. It's very tricky because they don't come up in that way, but we are always happy with what we are doing. Plus we try our best not to follow the graphic design trends."

Finding the balance between working for clients you "need" and the ones you want might seem quite hard at the begining, and if a significant amount of time passes and you still find yourself frequently daydreaming about being somewhere else, doing other things, you'll have to rethink your strategy.
Thomas Ulrik plays it by ear when it comes to picking clients. He doesn't have a specific set of principles or mission to depart from:

"Of course there will be moral and ethical considerations in most projects, but this is something I feel is necessary to deal with on a day-to-day level. I feel it would be completely limiting to personal growth and progress to have some sort of preconceived checklist that my work must adhere to—I'd rather like to think of my practice as being in a constant fluid state. The navigation between different subject matters is one of the things that I find interesting in design. Working for a fashion magazine can give you insights into things that can be interesting to utilize in a very corporate client setting, and vice-versa.

"One thing you learn rather quickly from working alone is how important it is to agree upon what authority you will have when taking on a project."

Many creative types are embarrassed, uncomfortable, or not bothered enough about talking about those uncomfortable things. For example, money; yes, it cannot buy you love, but it can buy you food, shelter, music, and some other things that make your life easier, or even possible. As much as you might not like it, money has been set as a standard for appreciation of human achievement and quality.

Setting your price right might be the hardest thing to do, it is not easy to calculate—and even harder to say out loud—what you think you're worth, but it gets easier with experience. If you cannot figure out how much something costs, ask your mentors and colleagues, or seek advice from design organizations. Even though every project is different, many organizations have a standardized "pricelist" which should give you an idea of how to value your work.

If you cannot evaluate the effort needed to finish a certain job, take some time to define your price rather than cutting yourself short.

Maintaining a good relationship with your clients is a bit like being a gigolo; you have to organize them in a schedule, have them pay your visits and lunches, and give them something no one else can, or else they will leave you.

Be professional. It will take them a long time to realize they have to trust you. Getting them involved in the process or at least talking to them about the design process will change their opinion and persuade them to trust your decision. Building this kind of confidence will prove useful down the line, because once your clients trust you, you will be able to influence their decisions or advise them better on questions of design.

Respect your clients. Thinking of them as annoying and ignorant obstructers of your harmonic (art)work process is immature and reckless, and will hurt you a lot if a client leaves you as a result. Remember that in your average day, every moment you step out of the office you're probably being somebody's client.

Clients need to be pampered. They need to feel special and happy about your relationship. After all, you are about to become an important part of their business. Be honest with them about what you can deliver. It's important to know how to set up goals and expectations for a project—that is, if you promise a client the moon and the sky and instead deliver a pizza pie, there's not going to be much (a)more. Designers tend to promise a lot in order to get the job, and then fall into the trap of under-delivering or being late. In other words, even though you're always pressed for time, calculate more time than you really think you will need to finish the job, and you'll deliver.

Chris Allen
Freelance
London
Chris works as an independent graphic designer in London. Since graduating, in 2005, from Ravensbourne College, he has worked with the likes of Spin, Build, Intro and John Morgan studio. Notably in 2007, he curated Print-Run, a poster exhibition featuring twenty acclaimed designers, held in support cancer research.
www.chris--all-en.net

In daily communication be friendly, open, and available during working hours. Define your working hours. Some clients get panicky, and feel inspired to pop into your office unannounced or, worse, call during strange hours to check on your progress.

"What the client wants is what the client gets!" was shouted at Chris

Allen recently. He prefers working with clients who find it more important to understand what they need is a good start, but not everything can be perfect!"

Keep your cool. Explain your side of the problem, but do not let a client bully you. If you start a relationship on the wrong page it might turn sour by the end of the first job. Be firm in your beliefs and prepared to argue your points of view on why your specified approach works. Avoid "I like it" as a justification of your creation.

"Setting the ground rules with a client depends on the scale of work," Chris continues, "but it's always good to begin with a demonstration of printing techniques and asserting a certain dexterity with them. Showing something tactile, whether an end product or just paper samples, it is always easier for them to envision this rough 'carved' form of what their final outcome might be. Once the clients are equally excited about the possibilites, it allows the designer to 'steer' the rules in the most appropriate direction.

I think clients can become scared away from trying something different unless confidence is converted into the belief that change can be positive. Being the visual creative, you have the

Photo: Chris Allen/art direction: Build Simple Records (Simple Records, 2007)

Your dream client is.../A client's dream designer is... (selected answers)

Someone who is excited about what they do
Is representing a moral cause
has a visual education and not tastes of my grandma
KNOWS MORE THAN I DO
Respectful and collaborative
Understands the value of design and the design process.
anyone who needs good design
understands that graphic design isn't fluff—it requires work and effort and doesn't happen in the blink of an eye.
ON YOUR WAVELENGHT
i don't know yet.
Beautiful, Rich & Famous
SANE
passionate and rigorous, with a little splash of madness
THERE IS NOT SUCH THING AS A DREAM CLIENT
willing to learn from me and willing to teach me
knows what they want but flexible in the outcome
myself: i wish I could design whatever I wanted, whenever I wanted.
STOKED ON LIFE
inmune to trends
Intelligent but not dictatorial
someone I can respect
HUMAN
nice and pays the bills on time.
CHALLENGING
it's not a PRIMADONNA
gives a criteria with minimal supervision and guidelines
my dream client is knowledgeable, appreciates confines of design relating to their product, and respect ~~what~~ that they've hired a designer to make design decisions.
cleary articulates their needs and desires
Informed, well-read, polite and sensitive
Enthusiastic, and knowledgeable about their product/service
one that keeps coming back
Stylish, Motivated and never Bald
sees us as a partner, not a supplier
INTELLIGENT AND DEMANDER
CURIOUS AND RISKTAKER

JUST A GOOD GRAPHIC DESIGNER
someone who exceeds all expectations
FLEXIBLE/OPEN-MINDED
someone who understands their values and works hard to express and comunicate them
someone who takes the weight off their shoulders and can make the right design decisions for them
has a vision and is reliable
HONEST AND EDUCATED
INNOVATIVE
hella talented
A designer that cares about the client (or at least appears to)
A GOOD LISTENER
someone who shares their visions
... reads minds and then does exactly what the client wants...
CHEAP, ON TIME OR EARLY, AND IS CREATIVE.
challenges but does not bully
Hopefully nice to work with and of course delivers
GOOD COMUNICATOR
FAST, INEXPENSIVE, AND ALWAYS ON CALL
ME
Lets them feel they are a part of the process, takes comments to heart and blows them away with amazing work at the end.
CURIOUS, EAGER AND TALENTED
an entertainer
A good counselor
Someone who listens to the clients concern and works within budget and deadlines.
SOMEONE WHO COMMUNICATES! OFTEN!
someone who makes them look good
A DESIGNER WHO IS ORIGINAL AND TAKES CHANCES
a designer(s) who produce excellent work on time and on budget to the best possible standard
has the mind of a child and the skills of 50 years designing
a good mix of creative force and business savvy
SEXY
Clairvoyant/Magician/Superhero
CHEAP AND OBEDIENT, YET SOMEHOW PRODUCES WORLD CLASS RESULTS

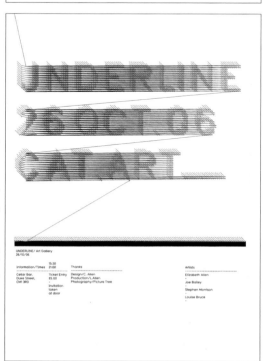

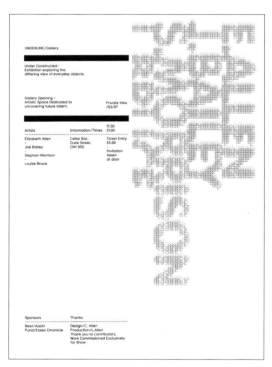

UNDERLINE/Gallery
24/06/07

16:00
21:00

Artists	Information/Times	Ticket Entry
Kevin Cortney	Cellar Bar,	£5.00
-	Duke Street,	
Josh Davies	CM1 3RD	Invitation
-		taken
Mike Mitchell		at door
-		
Samuel Thurston		

Sponsors	Thanks
Fund/Essex Chronicle	Design/C. Allen
	Production/L. Allen
	Thank you to contributors
	and their time help towards
	printing costs

UNDERLINE/Gallery

Under Constructed~
Exhibition exploring the
differing view of everyday objects

Gallery Opening ~
Artistic Space Dedicated to
uncovering future talent.

Private View
/03/07

17:30
21:00

Artists	Information/Times	
Elizabeth Allen	Cellar Bar,	Ticket Entry
-	Duke Street,	£5.00
Joe Bailey	CM1 3RD	
-		Invitation
Stephen Morrison		taken
-		at door
Louise Bruce		

Sponsors	Thanks
Beer/Aashi	Design/C. Allen
Fund/Essex Chronicle	Production/L. Allen
	Thank you to contributors,
	Work Commissioned Exclusively
	for Show

Chris Allen: Underline gallery (Underline gallery, 2006-2007)

UNDERLINE/ Art Gallery
26/10/06

15:30
21:00

Information/Times	Thanks	Artists
Cellar Bar,	Design/C. Allen	Elizabeth Allen
Duke Street,	Production/L. Allen	-
CM1 3RD	Photography/Picture Tree	Joe Bailey
		-
Ticket Entry		Stephen Morrison
£5.00		-
-		Louise Bruce
Invitation		-
taken		
at door		

sixth sense about why something feels good and why it is important, but clients subscribe to different sets of rules that govern their opinion of your design work. Bear this in mind when presenting."

Participation is always important, but clients who think they are designers are a special breed that will give you more pain than pleasure. Keep them away from the screen and find other ways to make them feel they are a part of the process. Being a successful designer means using your brains and skills to help someone else achieve their goals – it's their goals—and they have the right to be involved.

You need to make your clients aware of the fact that you are trying to do your best and that it takes time to make quality. If you see it's going to be impossible to meet the deadline, be sure to inform them in time.

Some clients have difficulties giving positive affirmation aloud, but if you get hired again, your client was evidently pleased with your work.

Do's and Don'ts

Do not avoid meetings and phone calls. Being available and capable of discussing the progress of a project gives your client reassurance and builds trust.

Do not be shy. Working will oblige you to meet a constant stream of new people, so you will need to get used to the social awkwardness of first meetings.

Don't give up on your ideas too easily, and don't be scared of standing your ground.

So what if they do not like your logo in the end? Going back to the drawing board can be a good thing. Your task is to listen to your client's demands and explain how your idea accomplishes this goal—simple as pie.

Clients like having the option to choose between multiple design concepts. Even though this might appear to be a good idea on the surface, it can ultimately be counterproductive. Your resources are often better spent refining a single design through multiple iterations. Multiple concepts often cause confusion rather than clarity. It is common for a client to request one element from one design and another from the second.

It is a standing joke in the industry that clients always pick the worst solution. This joke has gone to such lengths that some designers use a "built-in error" to coerce their clients into picking a better solution. Present only the projects you're really proud of.

Rumors
Studio
New York
Rumors is a multidisciplinary Brooklyn-based design collective formed in 2008 by Holly Gressley, Renda Morton, and Andy Pressman. It is a design practice interested in working with people rather than for people, and approaches each project based on the project's own conditions — be it context, function, or audience.
www.rumors-online.com

Sometimes Your Business Relationships Turn Sour

Sometimes clients decide to never pay. You might get tired of doing the same layouts after a few months, you might realize that someone is more trouble than he is worth, or perhaps a client is just plain unhappy with your work but does nothing about it apart from wreaking havoc on your nerves. If this were a relationship, you would have broken up. So end it, but be careful not to hurt your client's feelings even if you never want to see them again. In other words, try not to burn all your bridges.

You must summon the courage to be open and honest about the situation. Offer your opinion, discuss it, and give the client an opportunity to change.

If all else fails, use the old "It's not you, it's me" routine. Just say you are burdened with work and need to let them go, as you are not sure you can satisfy their demands to the standards they set. Try not to lie too much though.

It's easy to talk about how far your client is from being ideal, but before kicking him out of the door take a look at how you've been carrying out your part of the bargain.

Andy Pressman from the design trio Rumors appreciates "designers who are willing to open themselves up to what the client actually wants—not the client's taste in color or typeface, but the spirit of the project. A studio that will introduce to the client ways of reconsidering the project and its parameters, so that the possibilities seem clearer and more interesting. Someone to help a client bring things into focus."

It's more a certain type of relationship between you and the client, not what the client wants from you:

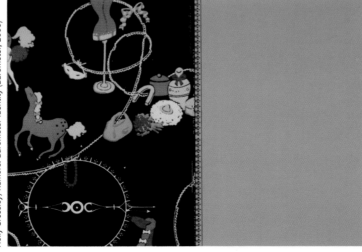

Holly Gressley/Rumors: Barometer identity (Barometer, 2006)

Growing Bigger

"I like it when the client can contribute to the whole thing, instead of just being like 'Yes. No. Yes. Change the color.'"

"It's good when you have a mutual understanding with the client," continues Holly Gressley, of Rumors.

Renda Morton prefers to have more of a stake in it:

"You're involved in something from the formation, not just something that's been going on, like 'oh this is a big thing and we just need to add an extra part to it.'"

Their favorite (and most fun) projects are the ones with clients that are new and have a vested interest. The studio then helps them develop their visual language and communication as well as their company.

When your business is booming and your clients begin recommending you to others, you will find yourself in a position of needing more personnel. Hiring people means becoming a manager, ensuring that these people get along professionally and personally for the sake of your business.

As a business owner you will choose how you wish to divide responsibility among your employees. Delegating duties to your crewat a sensible pace and keeping clients happy is quite a handful.

Give your employees enough rope to feel free and enjoy their work. Pay attention to individual personalities. Some prefer to be whipped into shape while others are fairly independent and reliable. Designers are driven by creative expression. So, if the jobs your employees are doing solely for money are strict and boring, find them a way to vent through pro bono or personal projects.

Managing projects and people are not the same. Listen to your employees complaints and comments, as most of them are concerned with the well being of the company in the first place. Allow them to feel as if they are contributing and making a difference in the organization. The more you

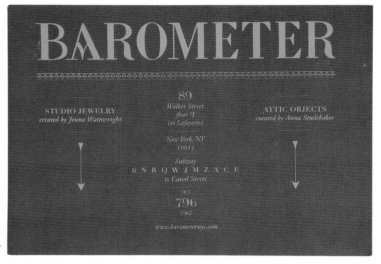

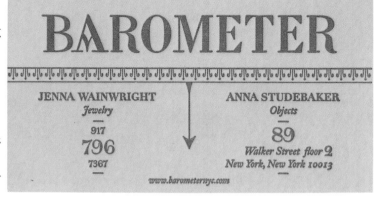

articulate your appreciation of their efforts, the greater their motivation. The more transparent your way of doing business and project management, the greater their feeling of inclusion.

The key to company growth is building an infrastructure of designers who can address the needs of a diverse clientele, leaving you to run the business and guide your people do their work. If your employees feel they are doing a good and creative job, your business will be successful.

Pick Me! Pick Me!

Self-promotion is not the exclusive domain of small studios or freelancers; well-known designers and studios also need to engage in effective public relations to expand their client base.

Apart from your portfolio you can spread the word about yourself through other websites or material you create with the specific purpose of advertising yourself, your product and your modus operandi. Self-initiated projects can be a good strategy, as they offer you ultimate control over what you produce and how you produce it.

Xavier Encinas from peter&wendy thinks this is a good way to show off your skills:

"In personal projects there is usually more freedom in the creative process. We recently released our first personal project, a type poster called 'Grotesque.' It was a good way for us to show our approach to typography and also the way we like to use it."

When developing your personal self-promotional piece be careful not to get carried away and waste too much time on frills and bows and drop shadows, as you might be damaging your clients by cutting short the project time for which they paid. Even if you manage to balance your client work and your personal projects, you still need to avoid overdoing it. Making your project too flashy and convoluted might prove counterproductive, as your client might be overwhelmed by your presentation and scared away by a perceived display of ego.

Even though his project brought him a lot of attention, Chris Allen admits that was not the intention.

Chris Allen: Underline gallery (Underline gallery, 2006-2007)

Duane King
Partner, creative director, and designer
Santa Fe, New Mexico/New York
Bob Borden is BB. Duane King is DK. Bob and
Duane are a multidisciplinary studio called
BBDK. In 2008, Shane Bzdok joined BBDK.
From their home office in Santa Fe, New Mexi-
co, and satellite office with Athletics in Brook-
lyn, New York, they collaborate with a network
of graphic and product designers, programmers,
and photographers worldwide.
www.bbdk.com

"I self-initiated a poster show to help raise funds for a lung cancer charity. Had it not been for my cousin who has lung cancer, I would not have initiated something now so important to me. I produced the promotional material but I kept out of designing a poster, as my intention was not self-promotion.

Self-initiated projects can help develop a house style, whether for purely aesthetic or methodological reasons. Providing the projects are diverse, I think it is okay for them to be demonstrated to clients. However, the client should never feel accommodative, these projects should always be demonstrated as a rather process of development than delivery."

Nourishing your pet project until it gets on its own feet and is ready to leave the nest might not be the first impulse for creating your stuff, but seeing it take flight and turn into something big and important can be very satisfying. Duane King from BBDK started Thinking for a Living, a platform for those who believe that, though design is a profession, it is above all a passion:

"It all began when I was asked to give a breakout session at the Dallas Society of Visual Communications National Student Show and Conference. I immediately began working on the development of a topic for this session and after some consideration, I finally settled on the topic of Thinking for a Living. Rather than being another talking head with a portfolio, I was determined to give the students something substantial to think about —a real starting place for a career in graphic design. In response, I compiled a collection of recommended readings and links that I had gathered over the years from various reliable sources that together illustrate the wide variety of tools modern designers have at their disposal and the breadth of influences we all should have."

Since that moment, the project has grown from the session, to a companion print piece, to a static site, and then on to what it is today.

The response has been tremendous:

"It has been overwhelming. Little did we know what we were starting. We have garnered a significant amount of traffic in a very short amount of time and have only begun to realize the potential of the project. We have assembled an international board of editors and contributors to maintain content quality and add new perspectives to the project. We are dedicated

BBDK: thinkingforaliving.org (self-initiated, 2007)

I Don't really think about them

they serve as extra points on your CU

They are good because they draw more attention to our field and motivate designers

Not always reflects the best work out there. I want one, no, LOTS.

Awesome, because I won one :)

Let's pat each other on the back for doing work that only we like.

THEY CAN ADVANCE YOUR CAREER

not really sure if they are relevant.

Flattering but inconsequential

They are good because some   produce incredible work.

i would like to see awards based on what positive effects a certain design/ad had for the client

they are good because they (should) set the standard

Important, because they show an annual overview about the trends in design

they're great, but very expensive

they are good, but maybe only designers look at "award-winning designers"

THEY ARE NECESSARY EVIL

don't see anything negative in them

they are great for fueling our already huge egos...

depends of the selection criteria

I'm only for awarding by industry values

Something that awarded to my passion and dreams

they don't matter as long as your client is happy with your work

best way to show your stuff to clients

they are for design snobs

i'm not a dog that does tricks for treats...

they're over-valued, but necessary

they are good to recognize good work, but it's not the most important way to be recognized.

I SHOULD ENTER BUT I NEVER DO

Personally would love one, and think they are great for the studio moral and generally kick butt creative spark and thinking into action

I think they provide a good standard of where the industry is, an the bar for achievement.

Mixed feelings. I want to stay away from them because I see them as kind of "fame seeking"... but who doesn't want the acknowledgment from their peers for a job well done?

GOOD FOR BEGINNERS OR STUDENTS

to the concept of open-source education and hope to fill a gap left in traditional specialized education by starting conversations and cataloging resources about 'the general' in design education."

Mingling amongst your colleagues is not only important for acquiring more insight through the input of fellow designers, but also to get new work. Duane King finds both reasons are equally important in this complicated, flat world:

"Technology smashes physical borders and creates new relationships between peers, allowing them to be collaborators as well as competitors. I believe that the new models in design studios, at least at the boutique level, will move to decentralized virtual networks that grant more creative freedom for the participants, incorporate the natural tendencies towards specialization, and allow for greater flexibility in scale and finance. A change is coming."

To promote your business you will have to be a bit of a networking animal, or at least a smart anti-social one. Get out to local conferences or business-club lunches, workshops, and meetings and meet people in the industry who need your skills.

Submitting your work to design competitions can also be a good way for you to grab some attention, although it's not easy for smaller studios to send their work to more significant contests since high admission fees are often prohibitive. If you don't have an agency/studio behind you (that will hopefully credit you properly) you might want to ask that certain client to cover some of the expenses, since it's going to be good PR for him as well.

Duane King considers design awards a necessity, but not necessarily good in every aspect:

"They can foster work that was generated simply to win awards—work that has no real connection to the public. It can therefore be fatally flawed as design is only finished when it's being used. Nonetheless, awards are a barometer of where you stand within your peer group and can validate a studio while generating client leads.

"Personally, I enjoy design organizations, particularly where they pertain to the promotion of standards and ethics in the practice of the business of graphic design. Unfortunately, anyone with a computer is a designer these days so it's good to have organizations that promote our profession as a craft."

BBDK: Packaging Design 100% (Soda, 2007)

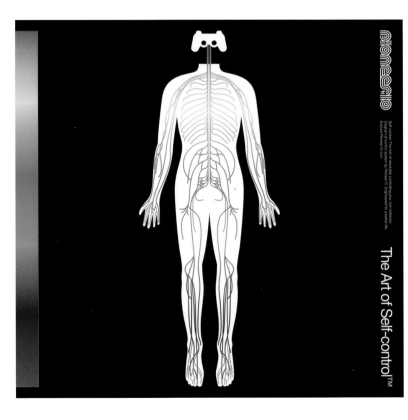

BBDK: GamePaused™ (Pioneer10, 2005)

CREATIVE BLOCKS ARE...

A part of my everyday life = 21.9%

Something I have to struggle
with every now and then = 54.5%

Something that I don't have time for = 11.5%

What is a creative block? = 12.2%

CREATIVITY

No matter how creative and spontaneously great and fast you are, there are days when nothing goes according to plan. No matter how hard you squeeze your eyes, ideas just don't come out, the cursor keeps blinking on the blank screen, and frustration mounts to a scream.

Can you boost your creativity? Is this something you learn? What kind of invisible force are you up against? Can you lose it?

Creativity does not go away forever; it likes to play hide-and-seek.

Even though it's difficult to be systematic about something so intangible as design, many creative professionals use techniques to bring them closer to an idea.

If you're lucky enough to work in one of the most creative industries, you'll probably also find yourself in a more stressful environment where people tend to burn out if they don't take care of themselves. So keep learning and finding new ways to stay motivated.

Optimize Your Creative Output

Troika: Newton Virus (self-initiated, 2005), photo © Dominic Holland

One thing you can't be taught, not even by books or the Internet, is how to create or control the "force" behind all of your work. This "force" makes you stay up at night tweaking that last block of text on a poster, making it fit the mental image you initially had while drinkin' juice in the hood. It is all in your head. Inspiration and creativity are a blessing (and sometimes a curse) that only the best have in unlimited amounts. What is it really?

Creativity, to merge a few serious definitions into a lighthearted one, is a strange ability to view things in a different perspective. Or, to be more precise, in more perspectives than one. To be recognized as truly creative you need to be able to rotate entire universes of possibilities and perspectives into new alternatives, each of them unique in their own special, unpredictable way.

Eva Rucki from Troika adds:

"Creativity is about thinking laterally and making new connections. It is about challenging the existing and about re-interpreting the past. Knowledge, persistence, play, and willingness to take risks are essential. There is no magic or universal formula, no process to be repeated and no guarantee of success.

"Working in a multidisciplinary, multicultural team nurtures curiosity and interest about different ways of looking at the same issue.

"Learning to trust and channel your instincts enables you to keep close to what truly inspires you and prevents you from being distracted by trends.

"Taking time to do nothing, to dream and wander without defined purpose, creates the peace of mind that enables you to notice, catch, and form the ideas that surround you."

Many designers complain they can't get creative enough with the projects to which they have been assigned. In a very few cases that's true, but then there are always self-initiated projects. And sometimes putting them out on the market can be a good way of attracting a new kind of work, the more creative kind of work you've been wishing for.

Eva continues:

"As part of our work we create 'new media' and new formats of communication, e.g., the SMS Projector or the Firefly display. Prototyping these new technologies is essential in order for a client to be able to imagine how it could work within their context. We put a lot of time into creating self-initiated work—free from any commercial restrains—which we often test in a gallery context. The bottom line is that you get contracted for the work you do and if you wish to get contracted for exciting work, than you have to put it out there."

To do all this you need to be inspired, which, according to Webster's dictionary, is: "Arousal of the mind to special, unusual activity or creativity." It seems to go around in circles. To be creative you need inspiration, to be inspired you need to be creative in the first place.

When you're in school, practicing creativity doesn't present a problem. You won't get fired for having the wrong idea and hopefully your mentors will push you harder to make something 'new.'

Andreas Grönqvist loves working with students because they are highly creative and unbiased:

"I love to teach students because it's so wild and spontaneous. The ideas are spinning off like crazy and they come up with so much more to work with, but they still don't have the basic knowledge and experience to tell what's right or wrong, what works, and what doesn't."

Perhaps your teachers were trying to show you how to be inventive, but you weren't even aware of it:

"In schools you learn to be creative inside certain boundaries and have to solve problems within them, such as math equations—but they seldom make you rethink and question what they are trying to teach you in the first place. It's more like: 'Here, teach yourself the basics and you'll probably understand how you can use this creatively.'

"The first day of college my math teacher said: 'I know this is boring and you haven't got a clue what you need these equations for, but one day you'll understand.'

It was high-level math and we did all these ridiculous equations. We got them right but we didn't know why we did them. Two years later I realized he was right, I could actually use that knowledge to do something creative, and since I was programming at that time I could apply it easily.

If you have a basic knowledge and a creative mind you can actually do wonders in this world."

Andreas' experiences span from working in big advertising and digital agencies to teaching small groups in work-

Andreas Grönqvist
Art director and founder of United Sthlm
Stockholm, Sweden
Andreas was one of the founders of Icon Medialab in 1996. In 2001, he started his own company, today known as United Sthlm, where they specialize in communication, identity, information architecture, and interactive media. Andreas' job is art director, and sometimes doubles as the creative director, and is always the one in charge of communicating with the clients.
www.unitedsthlm.com

shops, and even though people everywhere have different names for all its phases, the framework remains the same:

"It comes down to research, concept, design, and implementation. You can call it what you want, I even heard some people using a washing machine theme on it—soap, wash, rinse, spin—but still it's the same four stages of the creative process."

Anyone can learn this principle, but practicing it is yet another thing. Perhaps you think you can exercise your creativity by trying to make your layout as original and pretty as possible, and that's lovely since you're collecting artistic points as well, but given that you're part of a business you also need to learn to be creative in terms of handling your client. That means you need to meet the needs of different clientele, and different clients have different ideas on how creativity works. Having prejudices against them and thinking they can't assist you won't help you. You can be diametric opposites, having difficulty finding common ground because you work and perceive things in completely different ways, but eventually you'll get the hang of it:

"If I approached a client the same way I approach students in workshops he'd at least think I'm strange or talking nonsense because he wouldn't understand the level at which I was communicating with him. You can't get all crazy; take it down a bit. Baby steps. One little step for this guy can make a huge impact for the entire company. For you it might feel ridiculous but you'll seriously need to rethink your reference point otherwise you'll clash with the client."

At United Sthlm they work very close with their clients—instead of waiting for weeks to present an idea, they have one or two meetings a week and include the client in the process. Andreas' role could be defined as 'creative director coach for the clients':

"When we're on our own we do it our way, when we're with them they need to feel important and active while taking part in the evolution of the project. We disguise our routine a bit when we do the presentation so it feels as if they came up with all those ideas. Put it on a different level; *we* came up with this together, instead of taking the prize and stealing the show."

Andreas explains to us not all clients work like this; some of them surprise you with their suggestions, and they need you to go for them full throttle. In that case you'll need to switch to a different mode and just pick all the good stuff and try fleshing out what works best:

"Sometimes we're not the most creative ones. Some clients have really strange minds. In that case, use them, or otherwise help them."

To make the most out of them you need to learn how to ask (a lot of) the right questions:

"In an argument with a friend, instead of answering back and continuing the argument try asking one question after another. After a while the other side gets really frustrated because you've hit the core values of the argument.

"Same thing with the client:
– I want blue.
– Why?
– It's more corporate.
– Why is it more corporate?

"And continue like that until you've hit the core problem: Why have we come up with this? Is it really addressing the issue you have?"

Look at the target group, maybe that's not the problem.

Sharing ideas will help you develop them or get new ones. You'll notice some people hiding their ideas from others so they won't get ripped off, but that itself is sometimes a bad idea:

"I'm very happy to talk about any ideas with anyone. The old school thesis is don't tell anyone your idea because they are going to steal it. In my opinion that's not true. I have the idea and somewhere in my head I know the solution, the hard part is to go from the idea to the solution and have it all work in the end. My advice is to talk to your friends, try it out and trust that you have the knowledge and the experience to get 100 percent out, of it. Ask your nondesign friends what they think, as well, and don't take it personally and defend your idea right away, always think about why they are criticizing."

Share, and do it before you sit down with it.

United Sthlm:
SJ product strategy, concept development, graphical profile, structure (SJ, 2004)

Bertil.com product strategy, concept development, graphical profile, structure, functionality and graphic design (Bertil, 2006)

So-Called Techniques

There are days when inspiration runs dry and you stare at a blank page of something that was supposed to be your masterpiece. How did this happen? Can I cure it and be whole again?

Some people say you may. Let us start with supposedly the first person ever to systematize the creative process, James Webb Young, whose book *Technique for Producing Ideas* is a step-by-step guide to producing ideas on demand.

According to Young, it all happens in five stages. The first stage is preparation, where you dive into your challenge and saturate your brain with interesting source material, consciously or otherwise.

Once you have filled your head (and you do that all the time, exploring the new and curious world around you) you move to the second phase, the incubation. At this point, you let all this stuff in your head simmer for a good while. Supposedly your brain, otherwise strained to generate logical solutions to problems, when left on its own, makes unexpected combinations. The third phase, officially called insight, and usually called "Eureka!" or "Aha," sometimes even "I got it!" is when all this starts to make sense,

because you have made an unexpected combination, found a different approach, or a solution to the matter at hand. The fourth phase is evaluation. That is when you have to be strong and decide, under the cold light of reality, if your insight was any good in the first place. Go back to your research, test it against your audience, check if the message is clear, and if the chosen medium is efficient. In real life, you sometimes have to go back to the drawing board and start from step one again until you get it right. The final stage is elaboration. That is when you actually produce the idea. You have found your one true idea and you are sticking to it, because you know this is the one.

Brainstorming and Such

If you plan to work on a team, or to start working in an agency, you will soon come across the term "brainstorming." It was first developed in 1939 by A. F. Osborn[9], an advertising executive in BBDO. We define it as a group focused on the production of a large number of ideas, disregarding how much sense they make. No idea is turned down or deemed ridiculous; they are all recorded and built on, awaiting further critical evaluation in later stages of development.

not design related things
VIDEO GAMES AND INTERNET
analizing everything
SLEEP, FOOD
Photography, street ads, people, film, architecture, clothes...
coincidences
anything can be inspirational
my collective, unabridged life experiences
WEBNET
ramdom things, daily walks
DISCUSSING THE FUTURE
life, everything, 24/7
Anything and Everything that I find intriguing
it's a secret
MYSELF
sights and sounds
the street
My son
ALCOHOL
the city
Music, Sun and Vacations
Toilet
stock photos
My co-workers
observing my surroundings
Museums, Art Galleries
MARIJUANA
the noosphere
jogging in the early morning, music, my family & friends and the bible
the merchanized world
absorbing as much as i can and keeping track of what I like
LIFE EXPERIENCES & NOSTALGIA
culture, fabric, color Theory
ART, TECHNOLOGY,
LINGUISTICS,
PHILOSOPHY

at daylight" usually does the trick
Leaving my gray cubicle and looking
Bang my head to Rock 'n' Roll
LISTEN TO MY iPOD ON SHUFFLE
sort of genius leaks out when my mind is clear
clear them on my walk back to the studio. I sketch. usually some
I toon rocks off of a bluff near my house until my mind is completely
GYM
visual vocabulary and pencil sketches
BRAIN VOMITING
i keep a notebook by my bed as I fall sleep
feeling
Trying to visualize music wich gives a relevant
i dream of images in the shower
CAREFUL ANALYSIS AND PROTOTYPING
makes me more spontaneous and bad
I pretend that the deadline is tomorrow and the pressure
logically dressing it up
exponential circle growing a simple idea into more complex one by
ALCOHOL
THINK ALL OVER THE PLACE
the issue
have no method they appear after studying properly,
out when need be
I actively collect pieces of inspiration that I break
lay, keas to everything and the opsite the good one raised
go back through my collections and just let think ferment.
type uniformly and I collect ephemera like crazy so I
I start looking at the content and then start sketching, I draw
Taking a shower
LISTEN T MUSIL AND DRAWING
sketching, biking, and brainstorming
music, doodles from class, talking to myself
mind map
serious until I get what I call the idea click.
Sometimes i stare at the brainstorm along with related inspirational
doofing, and intense research.
Stream of conciousness free association manic craziness and
Research and moodboards
just sketch and research
creative logic
A SHOT OF TEQUILA AND PRAYER
personal experiments
to form in my head
I walk my dog in the forest a lot and that's when ideas start

You get inspiration from.../Do you use special techniques for coming up with ideas? (selected answers)

There are three critical factors in this process. The group must strive to produce as many different ideas as possible. All members must withhold judgment, as this could discourage other members from participating. Finally, the group leader must create a positive environment and channel all the members of the group in the same direction. If the participants are still feeling too uncomfortable to share their ideas without fear of censoring you can try silent brainstorming. Instead of shouting out your ideas, you would set a time limit for writing each down on a separate sticky note. When the time runs out, you mix notes from everyone in the group and analyze them.

There is an individual brainstorming process that works the same way, with several simple techniques to get the creative juices flowing.

Free writing is a free flow of creative thought within a given period of time. To accomplish this you need to set an alarm, sit down, and just write as many ideas as possible, in a continuous stream. Ignore grammar and all other rules; instead, generate as many ideas as you can. When the time is up, evaluate and decide. Rinse and repeat as necessary.

Free speaking is the same thing, but you record your own voice. If you are lazy, have bad handwriting, or want to move quicker, this is the technique for you.

Mind mapping is a technique where you draw a diagram of your associations, hoping to get more stimulating ideas from one. It is like drawing a map of your association process. Every idea is in direct graphic connection to the previous, so once you backtrack you can elaborate on the connection or even make new ones.

Word association is one of the techniques described by Edward Bono in his book *Lateral Thinking*. It is a way of creating far-fetched relations between random words and your topic

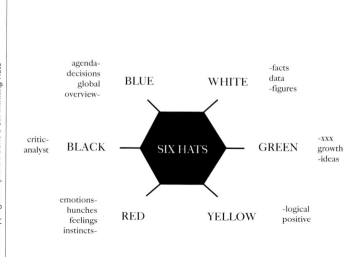

Mindmapping example: De Bono's Six Thinking Hats

or problem, in the hopes of arriving at original solutions or new points of view. Think of a random word (or just open a dictionary to a random page) and try to connect it to your problem. By diverting your mind from the actual problem, you will ostensibly make the "click" in your head happen sideways.

This and other creative exercises for lateral thinking are used in circumstances when our normal automatic perceptions and pattern matching keep us trapped "within the box." Shifting your thinking patterns is not always helpful, but when a good idea is discovered, it is usually obvious in hindsight. That is why you have to be able to scrutinize your work in an objective way.

These techniques are intended to spur your "design thinking," which is a problem-solving approach whereby you transform existing conditions into preferred ones, as defined by Herbert Simon in his book *Sciences of the Artificial*.[10] Design thinking is therefore a creative process of building up ideas, especially wild ones, as these lead to the most creative solutions.

Many companies are turning to design thinking for help when they hit the creative wall. GE, Procter & Gamble, and Maytag have made significant investments and organizational changes to take advantage of design processes and methodologies. Design as an innovative problem-solving methodology is fast becoming an imperative business strategy.

Don't forget that the flashbulbing bit is just a tiny part of your job. You can be prolific in your generation of random ideas, but you need to know how to focus and sculpt your results.

Mark Ury agrees with the phrase "1 percent inspiration, 99 percent perspiration".

"Ideas are easy. It's selling, producing, and implementing them that takes time and effort."

Overall, though, he doesn't believe in "generating" ideas.

"For the most part, the core idea reveals itself to you early in the process. You probably have to validate it, but if you've done your research and listened to the rhythm of the problem, it's "there" to be seen. That "moment" may have taken you ten years to get to—understanding that particular industry, psychology, pathology, etc.—but the actual idea arrives in a flash."

The De Bono Hats system (also known as "Six Hats" or "Six Thinking Hats") is a thinking tool for group discussions. The tool, combined with the idea of parallel thinking which is associated with it, provides a means for groups to think together more effectively, and a means to plan thinking processes in a detailed and cohesive way. The method is attributed to Dr. Edward de Bono and is the subject of his book, *Six Thinking Hats*.[11]

Role-Playing

We always tell you to put yourself in the shoes of the end-user, and role-playing is a "game" that does exactly that. You adopt a certain role with all its traits, personalities, motivations, and backgrounds different from your own, and think about how that person would act or what he would like.

One of Andreas Grönqvist's projects involves helping a betting company think like sports fans:

"I try to get them to know what happens when you go to watch a soccer match, why do they support this team, how did they think before and why do they drink beer before the match. If you are not a sports fan it's a really strange thing to do, but when you do it you start thinking in a different way. I find the term role-playing extreme so I'd call it more putting yourself in someone else's position, although I'm familiar with some people using methods that involve getting dressed up in costumes. A creative director friend of mine had the entire management team of her company dress up as women so all the men could get into the state of mind of how a woman thinks."

Perhaps in some cases this helps you get more insight, but in others it might just get in the way since you'll be too busy laughing at your colleague's wig.

Workshops

Another way of spicing up your routine is attending a creative workshop, or even trying to run one yourself.

Hort is a multidisciplinary studio that organizes workshops that give people the opportunity to break out of their daily routine and think beyond the confinements of their office desk.

HORT creative workshop

Accoding to Eike Koeing:

"Originally, we held student workshops at universities. As we love bringing the idea of Hort to people, sharing our experience and helping them learn and grow, we also began holding workshops for creatives at advertising and design agencies. The participants include art directors and designers as well as copywriters and even planners or accounts people. These people range from junior to senior creative directors to CCOs. We discovered that people really enjoyed working with Hort and the way in which we conducted the workshops was a real enrichment for their daily business lives. I [Eike] usually conduct the workshops, sometimes with help from other designers at Hort. Once, we also had our interns hold a workshop for younger students who had just started university. That was very interesting for both sides."

She also explained the pure Hort methodology:

"What we do in our workshops is somehow very simple: we work with the participants the way we work at Hort. It is the same process, the same way of exploring, creating concepts, designing, solving problems, thinking about clients' briefs and tasks,

developing ideas, etc. The workshop, as well as our way of working, has a lot to do with exchanging ideas, giving feedback, and helping to bring ideas or designs to the next level."

In their workshops they create an open space, free of computers and tight deadlines, acknowledging the importance of changing the way people think sometimes by being exposed to different environments, developing new creative techniques, and alternative ways of thinking and approaching projects. By making sure their groups remain small in size they create an environment where people are able to think creatively in an emotional way, rather then in an efficient or client-driven way.

The use of computers is strictly forbidden and, according to Eike, the people love it:

"At the beginning of the workshops they are sometimes confused. Too much freedom. But then they really enjoy it. They love going back to their roots, to everything they always wanted to do in graphic design. And the good thing is that they then try to integrate all this into their daily work at their agency."

Eike Koenig
Hort founder
Berlin, Germany
Hort began back in 1994, under the previous stage name of Elkes Grafischer Hort. Hort is a creative playground, a place where "work" and "play" can be said in the same sentence; an unconventional working environment. It is not only a studio space, but also an institution devoted to making ideas come to life.
www.hort.org.uk

Hort: Booka Shade: Planetary (Get Physical Music, 2008)

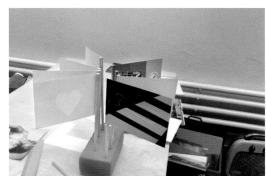

Hort creative workshop

Motivation

Klas Ernflo
Freelance
Barcelona, Spain
Klas is rather impatient as a person but usually works in the completely opposite way; he puts things together carefully and pays a lot of attention to details. In his little studio he works on illustrations, graphic design, art direction, and his own projects. He says that being Swedish seriously affects his work; he can't stand artwork that is too messy or too loosely organized.
www.klasherbert.com

For Klas Ernflo, motivation was a hard word to define:

"It's not really the money that drives me, even though I wouldn't mind getting some, but I've always been getting a lot of satisfaction from simply doing my work; drawing, doing things that feel meaningful, doing a lot of more artistic work—that's what makes me feel good. To be honest I think it's a mix of lots of reasons. If I had to choose just one reason maybe it would be personal growth."

Even though he sometimes misses the opinions of others he doesn't find it demotivating at all to work alone:

"I think my motivation comes from other things. I think its rather inspiring to be alone, to be able to do all the ideas that pop into my mind. Maybe this is just a phase, but right now I enjoy it."

Motivation and creative output are closely linked. If we defined creativity as the ability to look at things differently, motivation is the force that makes you go that extra mile to get to your specific solution. It is like possessing high intelligence—one must be motivated to improve and apply it.

Some people are motivated and passionately devoted to their work and show satisfaction with a job well done, happily overcoming challenges in their path. Others work hard for financial rewards, ego, personal growth, and status. You can find motivation in a task itself if it is enjoyable, fascinating, and inspiring. Many are motivated by professional recognition, but in the beginning of your professional life, fear is very often the main one—fear of rejection, ridicule, failure.

If you just keep on working, over time fear will be replaced with confidence. Confidence is actually fear that meets the experience you have gathered working, so you should study every failure and success in retrospect, analyze what you did wrong and what you did right, arming yourself with the ability to make the decisions again, but with confidence in your skills. You are expected to take some risks, but be realistic with your timeframes. Yes, sometimes it is necessary to work for three days without sleep, but do not make this your daily routine. As George H. Lonmer puts it wisely, "Putting off an easy thing makes it hard, and putting off a hard one makes it impossible." [12]

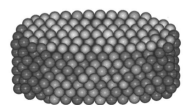

Vänder sig om & Koloni presenterar

Jens Lekman + Joel Gibb
<small>(Hidden cameras, CAN)</small>

Surplus people, Leif Elggren,

Kennet Klemets, Ida Börjel, Marja-Leena Sillanpää, Gunnar Ardelius, Karin Wiklund, Yo Amoeba, DJ:s Obra-Mia, Magnus Haglund.
Lördag 17/6 kl 19–00 Kulturhuset Underjorden (Braheg. 11, hpl SKF spårvagn 6, 7, 11)   100 kr

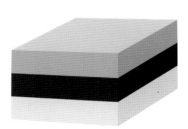

Vänder sig om & Koloni presenterar

Jens Lekman + Joel Gibb
<small>(Hidden cameras, CAN)</small>

Surplus people, Leif Elggren,

Kennet Klemets, Ida Börjel, Marja-Leena Sillanpää, Gunnar Ardelius, Karin Wiklund, Yo Amoeba, DJ:s Obra-Mia, Magnus Haglund.
Lördag 17/6 kl 19–00 Kulturhuset Underjorden (Braheg. 11, hpl SKF spårvagn 6, 7, 11)   100 kr

Vänder sig om & Koloni presenterar

Jens Lekman + Joel Gibb
<small>(Hidden cameras, CAN)</small>

Surplus people, Leif Elggren,

Kennet Klemets, Ida Börjel, Marja-Leena Sillanpää, Gunnar Ardelius, Karin Wiklund, Yo Amoeba, DJ:s Obra-Mia, Magnus Haglund.
Lördag 17/6 kl 19–00 Kulturhuset Underjorden (Braheg. 11, hpl SKF spårvagn 6, 7, 11)   100 kr

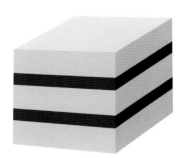

Vänder sig om & Koloni presenterar

Jens Lekman + Joel Gibb
<small>(Hidden cameras, CAN)</small>

Surplus people, Leif Elggren,

Kennet Klemets, Ida Börjel, Marja-Leena Sillanpää, Gunnar Ardelius, Karin Wiklund, Yo Amoeba, DJ:s Obra-Mia, Magnus Haglund.
Lördag 17/6 kl 19–00 Kulturhuset Underjorden (Braheg. 11, hpl SKF spårvagn 6, 7, 11)   100 kr

Klas Ernflo: Lekman/Gibb posters (Vänder sig om&Koloni, 2006)

Enough about fear, risks, and sleep deprivation. Now it's time to focus on the positive aspects of your work. For Andreas Grönqvist one of the most important ingredients in his recipe is fun:

"Having fun at work is crucial. I have to have a really good laugh at work otherwise I lose interest. And when I don't enjoy it that much the chances of getting the job well done are less."

Fighting the Demons

Every day is demon-fighting-day! Yes, you have a ton of minor or major setbacks that come with the package when you get a new gig, but the ones you set yourself are much harder to overcome.

Klas Ernflo confesses his main demon is his poor organization and planning. "I tend to be unrealistic about how long something is going to take, but as a paradox it is also one of my greatest assets as a designer. I'm never afraid of putting an enormous amount of time doing a piece of work."

It makes no difference whether you are a freelancer working from home at night or an in-house nine-to-five corporate designer; to be able to work you should be able to concentrate and hear yourself think comfortably and without interruption. In other words, have your workspace free of distractions. This means killing all your online chat apps and your phone and text messages.

Are you on the phone with your mother, chatting with your friend, watching an '80s video on YouTube or reading your favorite blog while preparing an important presentation? You say you need to be online 24/7 for research reasons? Having the entire world just an "alt+tab" away can actually do you more harm than good.

Make sure you minimize the distractions around your screen as well, even if it means dramatically changing the scenery. Paint the walls, get some books in there, and make sure you have all the tools you need. If you work from your home, invest time rearranging your workspace. Working in your pajamas can be cozy and can save time you would otherwise wasted commuting, but you might end up wasting even more time doing nonwork-related chores working from home.

Sharing an office with other people is always good, and not only because it makes rent cheaper. First, you feel guilty not doing anything with all those people working up a sweat around you. People meddling in your work can be a nuisance, but a certain level of competitive and friendly exchange of opinions can only be good for your work and for creating a positive and creative atmosphere among your colleagues. Being social animals, humans often need other people around to feel good about themselves or their work.

The folks from Ill-Studio work hard every day from early in the afternoon till late at night in an open space they share with other people so there's always someone around. Good for creativity and for preventing boredom, but the designers sometimes get too distracted by too much beauty:

"One of the companies we share our office with organizes fashion shows, so we are having hard time staying focused on our work while all the fashion week castings are going on."

All distractions aside, their studio provides an environment wherein its members' complementary influences meet, and contribute to the stimulation and development of the whole, whether the works produced are created collectively, or individually.

All ten of them share the same passion for what they do, even though they'd probably go to sleep earlier and eat better food if it wasn't for Ill-Studio.

Ill-Studio: art direction for Sixpack France new catalogue (Sixpack France, 2008)

Ill-Studio
Collective
Paris
The Ill-Studio is a group of collaborators devoted to fine arts. Their goal is to bring ten individuals together, working in various areas such as graphic design, photography, typography, illustration, video, motion design, etc. The studio provides an environment wherein its members' complementary influences meet, and contribute to the stimulation and development of the whole.
www.ill-studio.com

Ill-Studio: Nerdy Photos/Still Life Photography (self-initiated, 2008)

Never Stop Learning

Here's something you've heard a thousand times, but it won't do any harm for you to hear it again: we are all far from being perfect, everyone make mistakes, and as long as you've learned from them don't feel bad for making them.

Klas Ernflo went too far in his inspiration and admiration once when his poster ended up looking very similar to another illustrator's work:

"It was not meant to be a copy but I was too inspired. I'm never doing that again, seeing it as a lesson I've learned."

This is something people love to frown upon and be very loud about, but there are very few people that have never gone too far in their inspiration.

There were no negative consequences apart from Klas feeling quite uncomfortable and embarrassed when he was "exposed" by that client's former design studio:

"The truth is that I didn't realize I was copying at the moment I was working on it. I was just really into these French artists so much and I wanted to do something a bit in the same style. But I just got too close, and now I look at it as a good lesson learned...

I think it made me look more into myself for inspiration after that. It was positive actually, my work progressed after that and I made it more mine."

Mark Ury says there are a few key mistakes designers continue to make:

"1. Living in a design-only world. Every profession has the problem where its practitioners only focus on their industry. They read the same blogs, attend the same conferences, hold the same stars in regard, etc. A little bit of this is good: staying in touch, noting the trends, etc. But too much is like inbreeding: it generates bad DNA that replicates an idea or meme over and over ad nausea.

"Information has diminishing returns. You *have* to go wide instead of narrow: take in the world at large and enjoy and understand the issues that design can affect: business, politics, urban planning, social systems, etc.

"Better yet, I'd love to see more designers leave their profession and bring their skills to new groups; embed themselves in the environment. Otherwise, you get this faux-journeyman/Bruce Mau problem where you talk about problems that design can never solve.

"2. Mistaking the design process as a personal expression or art. Designing is a process, not an outcome. (A verb, not a noun.) Designers need to think of themselves as instigators, operators, and facilitators rather than embalmers of ideas.

"The greatest act a designer can do is to help others 'see' the problem or opportunity. Where they often get mixed up is thinking that design is a personal act, an artistic expression of the issue. In nonfunctional cases, like a literary book cover, this is basically true. Chip Kidd can be as self-indulgent as Knopf will allow. But 90 percent of the time design must function. It must 'do.' And designers who forget that, who affix their agenda to the outcome, often create more friction than they remove.

"You are an agent of change, not a taxidermist.

"3. Growing up. The design community coddles its members and greatly infantilizes them. An absurd vision has grown around designers as hipsters living in San Francisco/London/New York, reading Japanese magazines about Spanish architects making ultra-modern eco-homes in São Paulo, using irony to address every communication problem, "jamming the culture" by reading *Adbusters* and buying American Apparel unbranded T-shirts, and believing that ethnographic research and brainstorming will solve issues ranging from poverty to torture. None of this is true. All of it is a cliché. And much of it, if you fall into the narrative trap, will derail your best work. It's nice to be part of a tribe and speak their language. It's nice to participate in their rituals. But you'll be far more powerful with your skills if you focus on the ecosystem of *all* citizens, not just the ones who can discuss Koolhaus or kerning. See #1 again. Understand the broad world, address the real problems, and forget where you work and how you dress. Focus on your power to transform problems through visual thinking and design grammar."

Keep on Growing as a Designer

Teaching yourself to be a graphic designer is quite similar to learning a new language; at the beginning you learn a lot, you get bits of vocabulary and grammar and are overwhelmed with the new scattered information to process, but you're quite impressed by your progress.

In the same way that checking your work/experiments folder every few months generates a laugh at how far you've come and pride in your new creations—the progress is apparent.

Then you reach the point when your learning curve flatlines, and you need to learn more and step up the pace in order to move to the next level, and on it goes in cycles. But, with time the differences between projects in your portfolio become less drastic. That doesn't mean you've stopped making progress or that you are terrible at what you do.

Perk up. Attend lectures and keep in touch with your colleagues through events, exhibitions, design organizations, as well as magazines, blogs and forums (even though we'd encourage you to step away from the computer and change the scenery). Apart from bringing you more work opportunities networking also gives you insight into current industry trends.

To continue to grow as a designer you need to keep learning. New languages, new ideas—just focus on soaking up the knowledge. Make millions of friends from a variety of disciplines different from your own, who will expose you to tons of new ideas. Move to another town or just travel and meet other cultures and people. Read more than just coffee table designer books; even go back to school to learn a subject that is not your first vocation. Try teaching. As learning goes both ways, your students can give you new and wonderful insights into a world you do not perceive the same way. Make sure your job makes you learn new things every time. A person is intensely open and conscious at times of change, no matter what changes. So when in doubt, change something in your life.

Having other interests or a life in general is important for your creative work. It gives you insight into other worlds apart from your very own professional one. It has been said that all work and no play makes Jack a very dull boy, so hit the road Jack.

Go see a film, attend the theater or take a walk in the park. Let your mind wander away from all the pantones of the rainbow. Sometimes it is best to do something else to regain your focus.

DO YOU STICK TO YOUR DEADLINES?

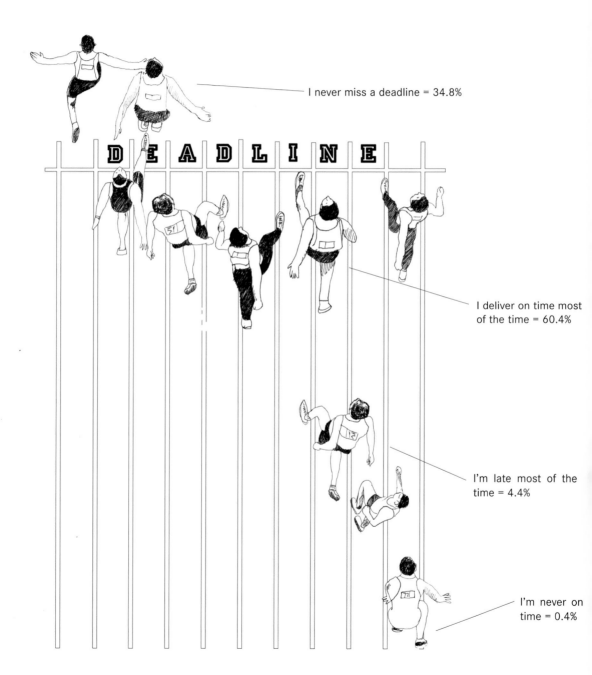

I never miss a deadline = 34.8%

I deliver on time most of the time = 60.4%

I'm late most of the time = 4.4%

I'm never on time = 0.4%

PROJECTS A–Z

Every project you work on will have the same variables defining it—time, budget, goals, and quality. All are interconnected and function in a certain equilibrium that you will learn to turn into your advantage if you want to realize it successfully from start to end. Once you've had enough experience you won't need an extensive checklist because you'll have the process in your little finger on autopilot. But until then we strongly recommend structure.

Even though concepts such as planning, organization, and project management might raise a few brows and evoke some sighs, they are absolutely essential for any serious attempt to stay in the game.

We are aware that most people have their own routines, that they work mostly with tight schedules and improvise their way through a project, but here we'll walk you through all the stages of a project—from brief to presentation—and touch on all the issues that might arise in between.

You Can Manage

Experimenta
Specialized studio
Wellington, New Zealand
Experimenta is a modern typographic design
and art direction studio, made up of Duncan
Forbes and Elaina Hamilton, and devoted to
modern typographic design and art direction.
With a subtle minimalist and modernist feel that
is very refreshing and unique, they are focused
on working with artists, galleries, museums,
and music and educational institutions.
www.experimenta.co.nz

Experimenta: Heat Like Me (Heat Like Me, 2008)

Managing a project is not about being able to create a complex spreadsheet to hang on your wall. It is not about to-do lists or scheduling meetings. It is about understanding the goal, grasping and making the most out of the context you're in and the technologies involved, communicating at various levels, handling stress, problems and people, and being organized enough to ensure everything gets done.

Start from the beginning, as every project should have a defined beginning and end. The decisive factors of money and quality and the pursuit of a specific goal will determine this equation. Managing a project means finding a correct balance between these three. In an ideal world all of your projects would arrive consecutively, one after the other, but this never happens. In order to maintain quality in all of your work you will need to learn to prioritize and take control of your workflow.

Once you have decided to work on a project, you will find a way to fit it into your schedule. Sometimes the motivation is money, other times it is the knowledge that a project could be a great promotional vehicle or, in the best of times, the project speaks to you and know you can do a great job.

Many designers fall for the Very Interesting Project Where You Get To Be Highly Creative But Sorry Won't Make A Dime On It (But It Will Look Great In Your Portfolio) Trap. Be wary, as Duncan Forbes from Experimenta has discovered:

"We worked on a couple of projects where the budget was very small and we ended up doing a lot of small fiddly pieces that just weren't worth our time. I think budget has a lot to do with it. You cannot be a starving artist all the time. Getting paid what you are worth is very important."

There is an age-old job evaluation tactic, used by engineers and supposedly first advanced by Clifford Stoll,[13] which involves a project triangle that many a creative person uses to determine and explain their pricing. It goes something like this:

The three corners of a triangle are *good*, *cheap*, and *fast*. (See page 156) It seems one can only travel one side of the triangle in his quest towards finishing a project. So a project can be good and cheap for your client, but it is not going to be fast. On the other hand it can be good and fast, but it is not going to be cheap.

scha Ed Rusch
scha Ed Rusch
scha Ed Rusch
scha Ed Rusch
scha Ed Rusch
scha Ed Rusch
scha Ed Rusch
scha Ed Rusch
scha Ed Rusch

Damien
Monika
Damien
Monika

You're
not
in
Guatemala
now
Dr
Ropata

Video Access Site
Video Access Site
Video Access Site
Video Access Site
Video Access Site
Video Access Site
Video Access Site
Video Access Site
Video Access Site
Video Access Site
Video Access Site
Video Access Site

The New Zealand Film Archive in your neighbourhood – locate your closest video access site.

(Shortland Street, NZ, Episode one, May 25 1992)

We're
takin'
this
bloody
car
to
Invercargill
boy

Video Access Site
Video Access Site
Video Access Site
Video Access Site
Video Access Site
Video Access Site
Video Access Site
Video Access Site
Video Access Site
Video Access Site
Video Access Site
Video Access Site

The New Zealand Film Archive in your neighbourhood – locate your closest video access site.

(Goodbye Pork Pie, NZ, 1981)

Experimenta: NZ Film Archive 01&02 (New Zealand Film Archive, 2008)

Clifford Stoll (see page 154) was an Ammerican astronomer, computer expert, and author. He received his Ph.D. from the University of Arizona in 1980. During the 1960s and 1970s, Stoll was assistant chief engineer at WBFO, a public radio station in Buffalo, New York.

The Brief

Briefs are knickers whose waistband rests at or just below the navel, provides full back coverage, and may have a high-cut leg. The brief we're more interested in is the other kind—the form in which the official start of a project is written. Briefs can be written or given in person, and sometimes even drawn up by the designers themselves. A good brief should contain all the necessary information on the goal of your work as well as predefined checkpoints and the actual deadline. Some of briefs are not very useful in the original form in which you receive them:

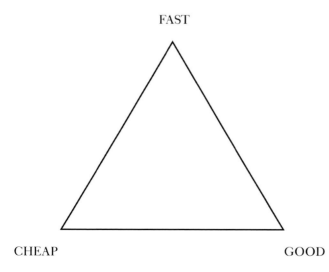

FAST

CHEAP   GOOD

Project triangle

"Some of those [briefs] are pretty loose. Real world briefs are very different from the ones you get from university. You are always writing them yourself, they are usually short, and to the point, pretty much whatever you can get from the first meeting is the most important. A lot of the time you will not get another chance to get more information. Projects just happen so fast," explained Duncan and Elaina Hamilton.

Every design brief should cover the key issues in a clear and concise way. It should give you a business background on the project. Who are the final users or customers? What are the strengths and weaknesses your client wants exposed or hidden? What are the strategic objectives of the project? A brief can be divided into the following elements:

GENERAL INFORMATION

This is where the client should give you a summary of the entire brief as well as some background info on the project. General info can contain data on the competition, market analysis, and suggestions from the client on the use of the media. It can be almost anything, from the atmosphere they want this project to create to the color scheme they want used.

TASKS FOR THE DESIGNER

It is crucial for you to get a clear overview or a list of all you need to produce for a certain project, be it a poster or an entire branding strategy. On some occasions you can advise your client to choose a different path or use different media for their message, on others you will have to respect a fixed set of values and limitations.

TARGET MARKET/AUDIENCE

Here, the client will try to explain which segment of the general population this particular design is targeting or to whom it should appeal. It can be a group of a certain age, gender, or marital status, such as married men in their forties. This data needs to be taken in consideration when thinking your design through, or presenting it, as it gives your client a sense of participation and shows you understand his or her needs.

THE SINGLE MOST IMPORTANT MESSAGE TO DELIVER

If design is solving communication problems, then you must know that communicating a lot of information simultaneously seldom works, as humans have a limited attention span when it comes to information served "on the go." Therefore you have to be careful about the amount of information you are trying to convey, depending on the medium used. Your client needs to specify the primary message, which should be visible in your design. This is often called USP or "unique sales proposition," and it should differentiate your product and its design from similar products on the market.

GOAL

What is the desired outcome of the project upon completion? Is your task to make people go somewhere? Buy something? Put the spotlight on your clients? Make this as clear and concise as possible.

DEADLINES

The most important of all deadlines is the date on which your project must be delivered. There are several checkpoints or meetings with the client during the design process, as you move from brainstorming to visualisation of solutions to production, and as the end of the line approaches, stress builds.

In most cases the client dictates the dynamics of the project, asking you to finish by a certain date. Don't let your client's demands scare you—it's up to you to be the voice of reason and prove how good things take time, while keeping in mind that nobody likes a designer who is slow or late.

Some clients will demand that you return a signed copy of the brief, treating it as a legally binding document. So be sure that the deadlines outlined in your brief are realistic and renegotiate them, if necessary, before signing such a document.

Sometimes there is no brief to be had, leaving you to create your own guidelines while keeping the same goals in mind, as Mark Ury does:

"After I've distilled the business goals, the competition, the gaps, etc., I prefer to verbally communicate the core issues/opportunities to the team and then jam. Sometimes the team has been with me through the whole process and they've done the same 'distillation,' so we compare notes, argue over the main themes, and then play around from there.

"Whenever possible, I try to include clients in these jam sessions, but this depends on the scope and style of the project. Engagements with small companies are easier to play around with: people are less formal, have less to lose, and can be pushed to be more adventurous. The larger the companies, the safer and more reserved everyone becomes. The design process is emphasized over design, and innovation—unlocking something new—becomes less available. (This isn't to say that big engagements with big companies can't be fun and innovative; it's just harder and less common.)"

Overall, his goal in this "jam session" is to identify core themes for the team to explore. Once you try putting yourself in your designated users' shoes, you'll be able to see from their point of view and create artwork that will appeal to the audience as well as your creative standards.

Getting All You Need from the Client

Things that need to be discussed but are not a part of the design brief itself are budgets and timetables as well as how communications will be managed or with whom will you communicate. It is very important to find a liaison officer—that is, a person within the client camp who will be at your disposal to dig out necessary information and further materials or references you might need.

Another important thing to think about is how much you will ultimately involve the client in the entire process. Will you split the project into several deliveries? How often will you meet? It isn't entirely up to you, since different clients insist on different levels of engagement. It can prove wise to involve the client in the early stages, as you might get to know them better, which will save you a lot of back-and-forth with your work. You might find the answers you are looking for by reading between their lines.

Dejan Dragosavac (Ruta) feels this issue in particular is a question of trust:

"It seems the most common problem is trying to make clear to the client the types of problems the designer might encounter, such as the motives and effects of particular problematic situations. The real answers reside in the question itself, that is, the extent to which the client includes the designer in his or her 'creative process.' Namely, if the designer receives material that is already structured and complete, his or her maneuvrability is seriously limited. There is no option for significant creative changes to work."

Pay special attention to your clients during the briefing and try to get the crucial points of the project right away. Ask all questions that come to mind, try different viewpoints, and gather vital information on time, as it can influence the outcome of the project. Finding out the day before the presentation that you were focused on the wrong thing could really make your life so much more complicated. As Ruta warns, sometimes it is the client's fault, other times it is the fault of the designer:

"On one hand it could be a simple 'I do not like it' coming from the client, or on the other a 'we cannot afford it.' Maybe the designer misunderstood the point completely? Regardless, there are only two viable options. Try to fix the existing solution or start from scratch, and I do not think that starting fresh is the worse option, as it often gives you an opportunity to make giant leaps forward, especially as you already know the material, content and special situations that arise from it."

Dejan Dragosavac (Ruta)
Graphic designer and studio founder
Zagreb, Croatia
Ruta studied in Zagreb at the Faculty of Graphic Technology. From 1994 to 2003 he worked in *Arkzin* until he started his own graphic design studio where he takes in clients mostly from the field of culture and civil society. His work has been published in a variety of design magazines and books, and in 2008 he received the Icograda Excellence Award.
www.ruta-design.com

Dejan Dragosavac (Ruta): Swarm Intelligences (net.culture club mama, 2003-2008)

Another puddle of quicksand might await you here, as this kind of a situation has a lot of potential to trap you in a never-ending-story routine where your client keeps making you go back to step one and expects you to change the concept over and over while paying you a flat-rate for the entire project. This doesn't mean you should charge your client every single time you open a file; better accept that it rarely goes brilliantly and smoothly from the first go (and if it does perhaps your clients don't know what's best for them) but let your client know your time is as valuable as his.

Framework

To be able to schedule your workflow you need to be confident about every step of the process, the available time, and resources. Outlining a sequence of tasks and their approximate duration per segment can be helpful for putting your project into perspective. Plan your work sequence according to your budget, deadline, and other limitations. If your budget is ample, but time is short, consider outsourcing some of the tasks for better results. If, on the other hand, money is tight, try redefining your concept so it fits its purpose without harming the quality of work you need to deliver.

Set yourself up with a realistic view of the expectations. Figure out the details of each project in particular as well as how they work in sync with other ones you have lined up and waiting.

Don't underestimate this part of the process for it will help you clarify, focus, and research the project's development and prospects, as well as your own.

A good framework will help you forecast the future, planning bridges between where we are and where we want to go.

Ruta concerns himself first with the limitations:

"From financial to technical (from how much the client can afford to my ability to create something from the received material). Initially, I try to be a genius and come up with a great solution in five minutes, but that does not happen very often—I simply become aware that these solutions are cliché or even archetypal solutions, which cuts this phase short."

It is often remarked that, to a creative person, limitations are often a blessing in disguise. It is better to embrace

Henry Laurence Gantt, A.B., M.E., (1861-23 November 1919) was a mechanical engineer and management consultant who is most famous for developing the Gantt chart in the 1910s. These Gantt charts were employed on major infrastructure projects including the Hoover Dam and Interstate highway system and continue to be an important tool in project management.[14]

them than to fight them; see them as a part of the design problem you are trying to solve. Each problem will have its own set of limitations. Work within them and you will soon achieve greatness.

This does not mean you should not create complicated designs or engage in visual explorations. There will be projects and clients that will allow you to experiment and create unique and complex designs with budgets that exceed the standard ones and allow more excess.

When you have these, savor and enjoy the project that allows you to do anything you want, but don't be fooled by all the bling, as it's so much harder to achieve something brilliant when you have all the odds against you, and the gratification is much more fulfilling.

The greater the number of simultaneous projects, the more organized you need to become. There are plenty of tools at your disposal for that purpose: online calendars, digital planners, and various types of charts and reminders in your smart phone.

One of the most popular systems for tracking your time and work is (get a brown paper bag ready) a Gantt chart. Named after Henry Gantt, who made them popular and available in the

West, this simple bar chart illustrates a project schedule, from start to finish, and offers a breakdown of the project work structure, making the terminal elements and summary elements of a project understandable and visible to a wide audience. The critical function of the Gantt chart has not changed to this day. It enables you to know quickly whether your production is on time or not.

You don't need to use advanced charts or fancy calendars to be in control of your agenda. As long as you stick to your own notes or whichever other system you have for yourself you should be fine. For example, Axel Peemöller is a lists person:

"I always have my to-do lists. Projects and things-to-do that are important are at the top. If the list gets too full I get really busy, if there are just a few points on it I slow down as well. I prefer to work on one project at a time, this way I fully get into it, but this is often not the reality. When I get booked by a studio I usually have to squeeze it in and put my list on hold, or do both at once. Right now I am working on two corporate identities, holding meetings for upcoming projects and my all-time favorite, which never leaves the list, tax income declaration."

The bottom line is that you don't want to screw up, forget, or be late. Axel can't remember when he last missed a deadline:

"I have been thinking about this question for some time now. But I never miss deadlines. I think one reason is that I usually estimate more time than actually needed. Or when I see that it might get close I tell people in advance and make adjustments. Or, if it gets down to the crunch I work all night."

Duncan and Elaina from Experimenta keep it simple. They use the most basic tools and try controlling the workflow:

"We trust our Moleskins, our white board, iCal, and Mail. Of course if you are ever in doubt just call the client. We like to keep the amount of projects down so we have more time to concentrate on the ideas and completion. Ideally we try to keep to two projects per month, but usually go over that (say four projects per month). But that is our ideal. We love getting deep into a project. Having the time to do it is very important, you can always tell a rush job."

Axel Peemöller
Freelance
Hamburg, Germany
Axel Peemöller freelances as art director and senior designer for design studios and clients all around the globe. Over the years, he has established a collective network of other designers, programmers, photographers, and illustrators, who he works closely with if essential for the project. At the moment, he lives and works in Hamburg with his dog, Bones.
www.de-war.de

Axel Peemöller: Tot (*Feld* magazine, 2008), KPMG (Meta Design Berlin, 2008)

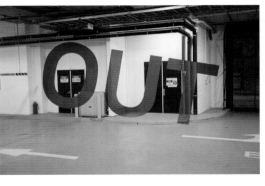

Research

Research often begins with the brief itself, as some clients tell you their preferences at the start. Even when given an extensive reference list of role models for your design, use them as a starting point only, as copying is no fun.

In the computer age, research usually means Googling everything that comes to mind—your competition, other design studios that have worked on similar projects—and rummaging through your own archive of projects to amass documents for further reference and research. The traditionally inclined can go to libraries or bookstores and invest in or borrow some books on the topic at hand and commit to reading. Whatever your path, you are accumulating material to be digested.

Working in a team allows you to dig out more information on the same topic, as every train of thought moves in different directions once it leaves the starting point. This can prove to be very useful—it works almost like a brainstorming session once you take out all your notes and compare what each other had dug out. This is how they do it at Paperjam:

"The thing that makes us different from most is that we approach jobs as a team from the start, but with a bit of healthy competition that eventually leads to one designer's 'ownership' of the job and sometimes the client. Our other distinguishing characteristic is our focus on research. Most of the hard work, the stuff that makes our work stand out from the rest, is actually done on paper."

Important questions to ask are: What do they want? What will they want in the future? What do they think of you? What can be changed about your

David Woods
Studio founder and partner
Belfast, Ireland
Paperjam Design is a small team founded by Paul Malone and David Woods. The company has been working hard in Belfast's cultural quarter for the past five years, delivering strong creative execution in brand design and advertising. At a push David would sum up their work style as a combination of humor, tangents, and accuracy.
www.paperjamdesign.com

Paperjam Design: Los Angeles, Members' Exhibition (Belfast Print Workshop, 2007)

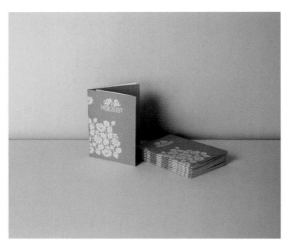

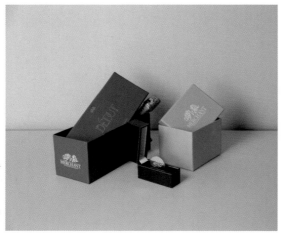

Paperjam Design: Merchant Hotel marketing/publicity (Beannchor Ltd., 2007-2008)

product or service that will make it more beneficial? What can you offer them that they currently lack? Is there a unique quality in their product or service?

David finds the more you know the target market the more likely you are to design something that will evoke a response, which is more important than the tastes of the client:

"As long as we have a full understanding of the job we will be doing I think we can work 'blind' to the personality behind the brand. For example, if we know the client needs a design to fit within a certain market, to advertise a particular service, or to introduce a new concept, then we can research similar companies and methods of dealing with similar concepts. The more you know the target market the more likely you are to design something they will respond to, which is more important than the tastes of the client."

All this information needs to be distilled to the core, when initial ideas pop into your head. Write them all down. For now it is all about quantity, advises Mark Ury:

"Across all these design disciplines and mediums I have the same message to designers: expand then contract. Fill up on inspiration and research and then play. Find connections, build them out, and make meaning. Then, step back, observe, and start to edit. Pare the system back to its essence. Expanding and contracting may take a few minutes, days, or weeks: the goal is the same, though. Observe, try, and refine."

Pixelgarten
Studio
Frankfurt, Germany
Pixelgarten is a small bureau for multidisciplinary creation founded by Catrin Altenbrandt and Adrian Niessler. They have been working for various clients in many fields of design including illustration, fashion, corporate identity, and editorial design. They are keen on doing their own self-initiated projects and have been very active exhibiting their work.
www.pixelgarten.de

Pixelgarten, David Hessler: Eigenes und Fremdes im Schuettelbad Digitalen Designs (Sebastian Oschatz/meso, 2004)

Pixelgarten: Um was es nicht geht (self-initiated, 2006)

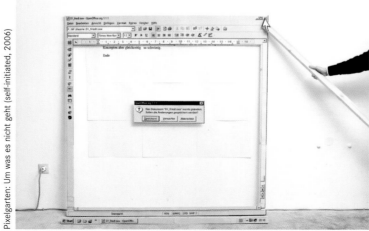

Get Your Hands Dirty

With the problem identified, all the research done and necessary information gathered and analyzed, it's time for the next phase—to mould your concept. The ideas are about to crystallize in your head and you need to let them settle and incubate for a while.

Catrin and Adrian from Pixelgarten explain to us how their process largely depends on each individual project, since they differ quite a lot from each other. Apart from that, the process also depends on the client, and the constellation you're working in, that is, your modus operandi:

"Working as a team is like a ping-pong match—one has the first idea, the other one criticizes it and develops it further and so on... the idea grows. When it comes to the execution, first we do a sketch and we think about the objects we are going to use for our image. The images are built up, similar to a painting. For the composition you add an object here and there, move it around until the object has found its final place."

Ruta, on the other hand, works alone, so when he encounters a certain type of problem for the first time he finds it is useful to check other people's notes and learn from older as well as younger colleagues:

"A good library is crucial. The Internet is useful as a source of information, but limited, as it gives no context. I used to develop several different concepts at the same time, but I have evolved to making a selection at the early stages of visualization. I try to give the client one solution. My experience teaches me that few clients like choosing from multiple solutions, and—the story goes—they usually pick the worst solution anyhow.

"It is equally important to set 'the point of no return,' when the client has to give up his right to radical change in the concept. The process of realization is relatively simple: how to create maximum effect with limited funds (and funds are always limited)."

For Duncan from Experimenta, concepts take a lot longer than the execution, although sometimes the concept is the execution.

"We have no problem making things look good, as most professional designers can do. It is getting a solid idea behind the work that can take weeks. Of course it's not often you have weeks. We like to have at least a week only doing concepts, re-looking over ideas. Depending on the work, we can usually get the artwork together very fast. Having another [designer] look over your work is so important, there are always things they will pick up."

When developing ideas, people sometimes get carried away by their own fascinations. We are not saying you should K.I.S.S. (or "Keep it Simple, Stupid", as the simplicity principle dictates) your personal preferences goodbye, but try to keep in mind your audience might have a different view. To assume everyone interprets an image or a concept in the same way very often proves to be wrong. Questions of semiotics can only be answered after some research on a relevantly sized group of people. If you are not sure, ask someone who is not immersed in the project idea to have a look at it.

At Paperjam, in order to keep an eye on quality, anyone in the studio has the authority to quality-check everyone else's work at any time, no matter what their position:

"We work with the understanding that the studio is judged by every piece of work that goes out, so our aim is to make sure each and every job is the very best we can do."

He gives us an example of a typical branding exercise to illustrate their method:

"Our first task will be to get as much information as we can from the client. We will organize a series of informal meetings to try to get the best possible brief. Without this we would be stabbing in the dark. At the outset of each branding job we put out a team of 2–3 designers to complete the first stages."

Stage 1 is always completed away from the screen:

"Our research is done on paper; brainstorming words, themes, and phrases, and then trying to tie them into three to four interesting directions each. We individually work these up and present them to the studio as early black-and-white concepts. From this, the studio decides which ones should go forward and be worked up into a complete brand presentation."

It can be difficult to know when you're on the right path, especially when you're working alone and there is no one by your side to tell you whether you're going nuts or whether you've nailed it. Ruta finds it a matter of experience and learning to deal with time constraints:

"For some solutions I just know that they are going to turn out great. However you mystify the idea of 'good

NYC
2012
CANDIDATE CITY

NYC'2012
CANDIDATE CITY

NYC
2012
CANDIDATE CITY

NYC
2012
CANDIDATE CITY

Gui Borchert, R/GA, Sagmeister: NYC 2012 Logo Proposals (NYC 2012 Candidate City, 2004)

Julia Hoffmann, Instructor: Michael Ian Kaye at School of Visual Arts: Space Magazine (*Space magazine*, 2002)

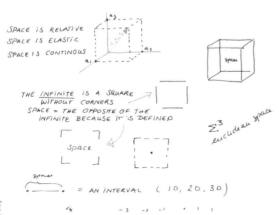

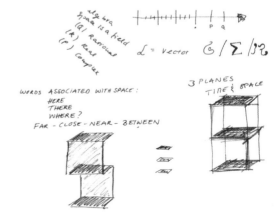

[space]

design' it turns out that, in the end, most end users recognize good solutions. Being able to view your work from many perspectives is crucial, especially being able to look at it from the position of the end user."

It's perfectly valid to follow a gut feeling, but you need to have logic behind it and know how to justify it to your client. If you don't find it, ask for help— borrow someone else's eyes:

"At the studio there are people to bounce around ideas with or show them what I intend on doing and get their feedback on it. When I work on my own this is different. Sometimes I get stuck not knowing if whatever I did was good or complete trash. Fortunately I have a bunch of friends who are great designers, so usually I ask them what they think and get their advice. On some projects I also get friends involved and we work more like a collective. I enjoyed this method the most. It would be great to work in a collective with other designers where everyone does their work, but, if needed, we can work together. Sometimes I miss being able to just show something real quick on screen and get a quick response to it," says Axel Peemöller.

Once you start playing with the chosen concepts, some of them will turn out to be unsuitable for various reasons (an inability to visualize them well enough to present to clients, insufficient materials available for intended production, etc.). Sometimes even the greatest concepts fail at the first reality check, that is, once you try moving it from your head to the real world. Learn to give up on them quickly and work with the ones that can be accomplished. You cannot afford to waste much time.

Depending on the complexity of the project, you might want to start off with simple visualizations, models, or simulations of the material you are hoping to produce. This way you can avoid wasting weeks of work on something the client completely dislikes; instead, show the client the direction you will be taking in the form of a sketch and/or a mood board. A mood board is a fairly primitive visual tool that consists of images, text, and samples of objects in a composition. This is where a picture is worth a thousand words, as it allows you to describe abstract values or ideas, and helps you develop design concepts and communicate them to other members of the design team or clients.

Wood McGrath
Graphic design and art direction studio
London
Wood McGrath was founded by Suzy Wood and Martin McGrath in 2007. The practice is concept led, and the work produced is often tactile, playful, and highly crafted, combining innovative production methods with traditional processes and materials. They aim to combine effective communication with an element of surprise, exploring the unexpected through visual, material, and conceptual means.
www.woodmcgrath.com

Presenting Your Final Idea

Clients prefer to see that you have sweated over their problem, so most expect multiple solutions to be presented, even if a lot of designers swear by one and only one solution. Bringing more than three different ideas to the table could have the undesirable effect of appearing unprofessional (i.e., not experienced enough to know what's the right choice) or confusing the client (who is expecting your guidance and often has no idea why he has chosen a certain path as the preferred one).

Martin McGrath and Suzy Wood explain to us that at Wood McGrath they don't have a fixed strategy for that:

"We usually present more than one concept because we usually have more than one idea that we like. What feels appropriate for one project might not suit another. We approach all projects with honesty, openness, and collaboration in mind. Showing more than one solution can initiate an interesting discussion, and can open projects up to new possibilities. On occasions we have shown a single concept if we believe it is the very best solution, but equally showing more than one idea can sometimes enhance the refining process."

Gui Borchert claims it all depends on the client and the situation:

"Sometimes it will be a requirement. Sometimes you really feel like you have more than one idea worth presenting, other times it may be interesting to show a range, and in some cases you feel like one is more than enough. What is really important is to only show something that you would be really proud to produce. That's a good rule to have."

Bear in mind that initial ideas need to be presented roughly. It's easy to get carried away and waste a lot of time on something that doesn't need that much of your attention at this point:

"In the concept phase I prefer to present rough ideas. By presenting the basic concept and the thought behind the design, there is a bigger chance for the client to get interested. Once you agree on the thought, you can focus and concentrate on the design and refine it," adds Axel Peemöller.

Show all the possible ways your solution can apply to life; if you're developing a visual identity make sure you apply that logo on everything from a business card to a bus. Make mockups of books or packaging; it will give

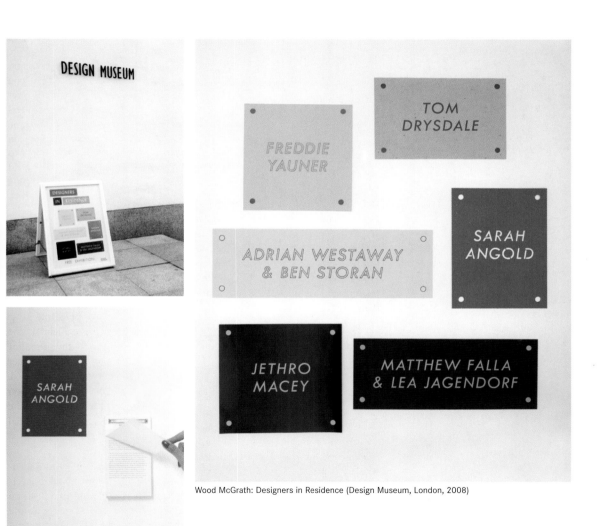

Wood McGrath: Designers in Residence (Design Museum, London, 2008)

your clients something to fiddle with and sometimes it will even help them like the concept, as not all people are capable of visualizing the feel of a certain designs from a picture on a screen:

"Most clients don't have a strong visual understanding, which means it's not enough to show them a direction, most prefer to see an almost finished design. Anything that helps the client to understand the design helps: mood boards, movie clips, songs, objects, scribbles, models.

"It hurts if you love an idea, you've already executed it, and you think it looks amazing but the client doesn't."

Although it is true that a good design should speak for itself, it still needs to be presented to the client. Yet, even though they are as proud and convinced by their work as they can be, many designers freeze once they have an audience.

Learn to tell stories. Putting together coherent sentences without a lot of *ummming, errrrring* means a lot. If you trust your work it will show, and a little confidence can go a long way. Show them your process and how you arrived at your idea, talk them through the design, explaining how it meets the needs of their users and business objectives. Be open and honest. Show them how hard you worked without being literal, and they will love you for your passion. More important, the communication will help them understand how you work and just how solid the foundation of your idea is.

Stop worrying. What's the worst that can happen? Your client might send you back to the drawing board, the plan B you prepared as contingency might fail, or you simply might never find a common language. Ask more questions if their feedback strikes you as cryptic or unintelligible; it might be important for the outcome of the project. Namely, the client could have insight into something you never thought of (especially if you have no experience in a specific market).

Think twice before indulging a client's taste at the expense of the project's quality. Your ultimate goal is to produce the best product possible, not stroke the ego of the client. One of the main problems you could encounter with your initial presentations will be finding the right person to present your work to. There is nothing worse than jumping through flaming hoops in front of a group of people who in the end just forward your work to a decision maker without any explanation. Make   an   effort   to   find   the

sketchbook, sewing machine, cutter

my memory

LIGHTBOX

Sketchbook, Bulldog clips, Spray-mount

paperclips, elastic

Beer coasters.

my boyfriend the artist

post-its and a sketchbook, pen ink and a scanner

Sketchbook and notepad and water bottle

the back of proof prints outs...

I NEVER REALLY USE PAPER to "SKETCH IDEAS"

a notepad, a doodle book, a mini-dry erase board and clip boards

MAGIC WHITEBOARD

Doodles and notes on the back of my hand

I Build my own tools, write software, etc ...

Sketchbooks and my camera

napkins

PHOTOCOPIER

collages

people who make the decisions and present to them alone. Use these magic words: "It will save everyone time and money."

If your presentations are foundering a lot, there could be a good reason for it. Perhaps you haven't been paying enough attention to the client or he failed to reveal information crucial to the project on time:

"It is hard to define what is the most valuable feedback or information. On one hand, it could be a simple 'I do not like it' coming from the client, or on the other a 'we cannot afford it.' Maybe the designer misunderstood the point completely?

"Regardless, there are only two viable options. Try to fix the existing solution or start from scratch, and I do not think that starting fresh is the worse option, as it often gives you an opportunity to make giant leaps forward, especially as you already know the material/content and special situations that arise from it," says Ruta.

Gui Borchert thinks the worst that could happen is actually what happens before a brief is even assigned—working with the wrong client.

"Great work comes from great clients. Of course that isn't always the case,

and we will always do our best to create the best possible work and sell it, but sometimes that becomes impossible, and that is when you have to decide how much you are going to compromise before it's not worth it anymore. I think the plan B is to understand exactly why the client wasn't happy and what needs to be different for the next round. Communicating is very important at that point, knowing the right time to listen and the right time to talk, and picking the right battles. And then afterwards put it all together, see what's left in the table, and evaluate what the right thing to do next is."

Production

So, it all went smoothly. The client bought your idea, perhaps after a few corrections, and now you have to make it real. This may seem easy, but there are many traps that await you on the road to fruition.

Most of the time the task of fact checking and proofreading belongs to someone else, while your job is to make sure your design reaches its destination spotless. God is in the details, no matter which medium you're working in—print, Web, or whatever.

If you have two versions of a photo, the wrong one will make its way to the printer. Blueline proofs reveal previously invisible errors. This is Murphy's Law in all of its erroneous glory. If things can go wrong, they will.

"If we are at the point of sending our materials to print, then aesthetic dilemmas are the thing of the past and we are dealing with practical/technical issues." Ruta tries to think like a printer, determine what issues might arise and what could go wrong, because the printer has his own worries and he should not be burdened with his problems.

Do not be sloppy and do not expect anyone else to be your quality control. Check, re-check and then check your files again before sending them to the printer. This is still cheaper than reprinting the entire series.

The people at Paperjam have their own method of preventing disasters that can be avoided:

"A huge amount of our work is printed, so there is a studio-wide checklist that each designer must follow before a job goes to print: making sure the color profiles are correct, page sizes and counts are as specified, photos are the right resolution, and colour settings and fonts are included. These are the things that can turn a great job into a terrible one and a happy client into a stressed one."

If possible, have your printer make a test print. Verify that all the elements are in place, run it by your client, and, if everything is okay, proceed. Though hanging out at the printer's workspace, getting high off the fumes produced by the heavy machinery and chemicals, may not seem like the best use of your time, in more delicate printing processes your presence might be more than valuable. If something goes wrong you can notice it on the spot and shout those magical words: "Stop the press!"

Paying attention to detail is universal, but slightly different principles apply across different media. Before a website is launched, it must undergo thorough testing.

There is always room for improvement. Make sure you build things so they can grow without having to be rebuilt. This means that the structure of your website should be thought out and, if possible, modular, allowing expansion in other directions for the further needs of your clients. It also means that you should never launch a website on a Friday or in the middle of the night, for obvious reasons.

Evaluation and Reflection

After days/weeks/months of wrestling with a project, you've finally finished it. You might even miss the buzz and turmoil it injected into your daily routine. Are you happy? Relieved? Or perhaps feeling used and abused? Was it worth the effort, and did your design achieve its goal?

Sometimes you'll feel like raising your hands in the air with joy and shouting from a rooftop, other times you'll feel like a deflated balloon that just hit a wall, but if you want to stay in the race you won't have time for any of that because you'll already be knee-deep in your next assignment.

Even if you're in a rush to get new things done, try not to sweep this task under the carpet as soon as your client is out of sight. Evaluation is necessary at the completion of every project, allowing you to reflect on your mistakes so you don't repeat them.
Give yourself some time, let things simmer down, then address these two main points when trying to evaluate your work: what have you achieved with this project, and what has this project done for your client?

For you personally, ideally at the end of each chapter you'd find you've learned something from the work, acquired new skills, techniques, or grasped new concepts through the creative process. Each piece of work you undertake should build on your existing knowledge and understanding of art and design, leaving you better equipped for your next challenge.

Client-side results cannot be fully evaluated without feedback from the client. In order to develop a better and meaningful relationship, if possible, try to meet the clients after the project concludes with the purpose of gathering information about the performance of the product and the experience of working with your studio.

If you've been working in a team it would be desirable to go through the evaluation process with them, not only for pinning down things that went good or bad in production, but also for determining the way you function as a group.

If you're running a studio, you have a greater responsibility toward your employees; feel their pulse, see how they feel about what they've accomplished, and reward them.

"Working in a disciplined way is easy if you enjoy what you do," says Martin McGrath from Woods McGrath.

"Running a studio requires a great deal of dedication and commitment, so it is unthinkable that one would commit to doing so unless you're prepared to put in a lot of hard work."

There are times when, for various reasons, despite all the effort, the meetings and the blood, sweat, and beers, things just do not work out. David Woods from Paperjam has had some "jams" to share in that department:

"Invariably, with five years worth of work, there have been projects that for one reason or another have failed to leave our studio or have not worked as well as we would have hoped when they have gone out to the public. We do try to partner ourselves with clients who understand that we have their very best interests at heart, and that we really do know what we are doing, but this is not always reciprocated and this is probably where these jobs fall down."

He thinks there is sometimes a lack of understanding of what a design studio does, and the growth of desktop publishing packages has meant that most people believe design is just a matter of getting good at using computers, rather than learning an important skill:

"We have had brand projects that we were extremely excited about fail very quickly because the clients have not understood that a logo needs to be used on more than just a letterhead. We have seen logo designs used on two or three items and then disappear."

Don't take it personal, chalk it up to experience. Soon other projects will come, and you'll have plenty of opportunities to do things better. Everyone has to learn to deal with an occasional failure, and so will you.

We'll wrap it up with a piece of advice from Martin and Suzy at Wood McGrath:

"Work hard, be patient, and treat clients, contemporaries, suppliers, and associates with the respect they deserve. The work you make relies on good relationships with all of these people."

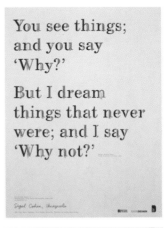

Wood McGrath: IYDEY Award (British Council, 2007)

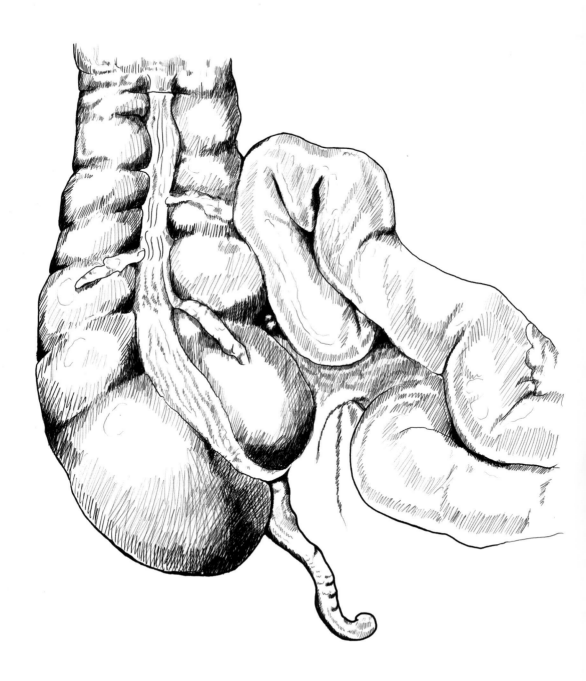

APPENDIX

The checklist

Naming Documents and Folders

This might sound obvious, but you should name your files and folders in such a way that you know what they contain without opening them. You might think you have your own perfect little system and you always know your way around it, but when someone else opens your files they won't have so much fun wasting time on deciphering whether the final file is CompanyBranding-last.* or CompanyBranding-reallyfinal.* or CompanyBranding-finalfinal.* Once you start moving your layers around your document, name them accordingly using the same principle.

The same applies to folders. Every project should get a folder with a clear name, every segment of the project should get its own folder, and they all should get named in the same clear and understandable manner.

Quality Control

When you are done, always ask someone who is not working on the same project to have a look, because being immersed in a project makes you naturally blind to obvious mistakes.

Once your project is completed and ready for press, ensure you have given precise specifications to the production people. Just before the document is sent to a printer, repeat these specifications yet again to avoid mistakes.

Special care should be applied to document dimensions (is it a standard printing format or does it spill from the side of the screen if it is a Web project?), photograph dimensions, and the resolution and sharpness of the photographs (unsharp, undo). Be careful to send your file in the color mode (RGB, CMYK, B/W, Greyscale) that corresponds with your publishing medium.

Place your markers in every document. Check them again before sending to print.

Look out for the distance of design elements from the edge of the document and if a document needs special treatment, such as cutting, laser drilling, hole punching, or other fancy stuff. Pay attention to the technical requirements of a certain technique (the thickness of the cutting tool, for example) as these might screw up your superbly refined idea.

If you are press cutting your paper or using any other kind of post-print work on it, pay attention to technical details involved in the process, like the thickness of the cutting knife, so you can prepare your work accordingly (with more than 3 mm spacing between the lines). Your typography should be checked carefully as well. Some printing techniques make certain small-point type illegible, so double-check the sizes. Be careful to use unicode versions of fonts to avoid problems, get rid of double fonts, and set your grid properly.

Always print out a version of your design, preferably in 1:1 ratio if possible. Make a model for every complex graphic material to be able to check for possible problems before it gets produced. Ask your printer to make you a test print or a match print.

In Adobe Veritas

If the application you work in allows it, use .psd or .ai files as links. If you just copy-paste it all in the same file, corrections will be a lot more difficult.

Once you start moving your layers around in PS or AI, name and group them accordingly to make it easier for others to navigate through them.

When working on larger projects (meaning multiple pages), be sure to create a master page to make it easier on yourself later in the process. The same applies to typography. Create your character styles, paragraph styles, and indents. Yes, it takes some time to make those, but once you have to go back to a certain file it will be worth it.

Archive

When a project is completed, taking up a lot of space on your machine, archive it. It does not matter if you use an external medium (CD, DVD) or a spare hard disk, keeping your projects tidy means getting rid of all of the stuff that is no longer needed. If you are keen to keep some aspects from your experimenting that you think are recyclable, simply create a universal folder for your rejected proposals, otherwise you'll never remember to look through the old files.

If you have made a model or have a copy of the actual produced material, take a photograph (or a series of photographs) of the project to add to your portfolio, to show to clients, or to have handy when some editor wants to feature your work in some design book. Do this sooner rather than later, as samples get lost, dirty, and broken before you know it.

Bibliography

1. Bureau of Labor Statistics, U.S. Department of Labor: *Occupational Outlook Handbook: Graphic Designers*, 2008–09 edition, <www.bls.gov/oco/ocos090.htm>. [Visited: June 18, 2008].

2. Smith, Adam: *The Division of Labor*, <www.wsu.edu/~dee/ENLIGHT/WEALTH1.HTM>. [Visited: June 21, 2008].

3. TNS: *TNS Media Intelligence Forecasts 2.6 Percent Increase in U.S. Advertising Spending for 2007*, <http://www.tns-mi.com/news/01082007.htm>. [Visited: June 28, 2008] .

4. PWC: *Global Entertainment and Media Outlook: 2008-2012*, <http://www.pwc.com/extweb/pwcpublications.nsf/docid/5AC172F2C9DED8F5852570210044EEA7?opendocument&vendor=none>. [Visited: June 28, 2008].

5. Nielsen, Jakob: *Jakob Nielsen's Alertbox*, <www.useit.com/alertbox/features.html>. [Visited: July 2, 2008].

6. Saffer, Dan: *Ethics in Design*, <www.odannyboy.com/blog/cmu/archives/000776.html>. [Visited: June 10, 2008].

7. Bierut, Michael: *Will the Real Ernst Bettler Please Stand Up?*, <do3.rubystudio.com/archives/entry.html?id=31066>. [Visited: July 2, 2008].

8. Tiplady, Rachel: *From Faux to Fortune*, <www.businessweek.com/magazine/content/05_46/b3959136.htm>. [Visited: June 7, 2008].

9. *Biography Research Guide: Alex Faickney Osborn*, <http://www.123exp-biographies.com/t/00031031532/>. [Visited: July 6, 2008].

10. Simon, Herbert: *The Sciences of the Artificial*, 3rd edition, Cambridge, MIT PRESS, 1996.

11. *Edward De Bono's Web*, <www.edwdebono.com/debono/debonoi.htm>. [Visited: June 6, 2008].

12. *Quotes by George H. Lonmer*, <www.answers.com/topic/lonmer-george-h>. [Visited: June 8, 2008].

13. Stoll, Clifford: *Silicon Snake Oil: Second Thoughts on the Information Highway*, 1st edition, New York, Doubleday, 1995.

14. *Gantt Charts*, <www.ganttchart.com/History.html>. [Visited July 6, 2008].

Recommended reading

Aaker, David A.: *Building Strong Brands*, London, Simon & Schuster, 2002.

Albers, Josef: *Interaction of Color*, reviewed and expanded edition, New Haven, Conn.,Yale University Press, 2006.

Arden, Paul: *It's Not How Good You Are, It's How Good You Want To Be*, London, Phaidon, 2003.

Ash, Jared; Gurianova, Nina; Janecek, Gerald; Rowell, Margit: *The Russian Avant-Garde Book: 1910-1934*, New York, The Museum of Modern Art, 2002.

Banksy: *Wall and Piece*, London, Random House, 2006.

Berger, Josh; Dougher, Sarah; Plazm: *100 Habits of Successful Graphic Designers*, Gloucester, Mass., Rockport Publishers, 2005.

Bierut, Michael; Drenttel, William; Heller, Steven: *Looking Closer 5: Critical Writings on Graphic Design,* New York, Allworth, 2007.

Bierut, Michael: *Seventy-nine Short Essays on Design*, 1st edition, New York, Princeton Architectural Press, 2007.

Broos, Kees; Crouwel, Wim: *Alphabets*, Corte Madera, Gingko Press, 2003.

De Bono, Edward: *Six Thinking Hats*, revised edition, London, Penguin, 2000.

Evamy, Michael: *Logo*, London, Laurence King Pub. Ltd., 2007.

Fletcher, Alan: *The Art of Looking Sideways*, London, Phaidon, 2007.

Hara, Kenya: *Designing Design*, Baden, Lars Müller Publishers, 2007.

Heller, Steven; Balance, Georgette: *Graphic Design History*, New York, Allworth Press, 2001.

Heller, Steven; Talarico, Lita: *The Design Entrepeneur: Turning Graphic Design into Goods that Sell,* Beverly, Mass., Rockport Publishers, 2008.

Heller, Steven: *Design Literacy: Understanding Graphic Design*, 2nd edition, New York, Allworth Press, 2004.

Hollis, Richard: *Graphic Design: A Concise History*, reviewed and expanded edition, New York, Thames & Hudson, 2002.

Jenks, Chris: *Visual Culture*, London [u.a.], Routledge, 2001.

Johnson, Michael: *Problem Solved*, London, Phaidon, 2002.

Johnson, Steven: *Everything Bad is Good for You*, New York, Riverhead Books, 2005.

KesselsKramer: *2 Kilo of KesselsKramer*, Tokyo, PIE Books, 2005.

Kidd, Chip; Updike, John: *Chip Kidd: Book One: Work: 1986-2006*, New York, Rizzoli, 2005.

Kroeger, Michael; Rand, Paul: *Paul Rand: Conversations with Students*, New York, Papress, 2008.

Lasn, Kalle: *Design Anarchy*, Freiburg, Orange Press, 2006.

Lupton, Ellen; Phillips, Jennifer C: *Graphic Design: The New Basics*, New York, Princeton Architectural Press, 2008.

Lynch, David: *Catching the Big Fish: Meditation, Consciousness, and Creativity*, 1st trade paperback edition, New York, Tarcher, 2007.

Mason, Daniel: *Materials, Process, Print: Creative Ideas for Graphic Design*, London, Laurence King, 2007

Millman, Debbie: *How to Think Like a Great Graphic Designer*, New York, Allworth Press: School of Visual Arts, 2007.

Monguzzi, Bruno; Berger, Maurice; Nunoo-Quarcoo, Franc: *A Designers Perspective*, Baltimore, Center for Art and Visual Culture, UMBC, 1999.

Müller-Brockmann, Josef; Müller-Brockmann, Shizuko: *History of the Poster*, London, Phaidon, 2004.

Müller-Brockmann, Josef: *A History of Visual Communication*, Niederteufen, Arthur Niggli, 1986.

Müller-Brockmann, Josef: *Grid Systems in Graphic Design*, 4th revised edition, Sulgen, Verlag Niggli, 1996.

Müller-Brockmann, Josef: *The Graphic Artist and his Design Problems*, 3rd edition, Santa Monica, Calif., Ram Publications, 2003.
Munari, Bruno: *Design as Art*, London, Penguin, 2008.

Nunoo-Quarcoo, Franz: Paul Rand: *Modernist Designer*, Baltimore, University of Maryland, 2003.

Olins, Wally: *The Brand Handbook*, London, Thames & Hudson, 2008.

Potter, Norman: *What is a Designer*, 4th edition, London, Hyphen Press, 2002.

Print Work: An Exploration of Printing Techniques, Hong Kong, Victionary, 2008.

Sagmeister, Stefan: *Things I Have Learned in my Life so Far*, Mainz, Schmidt, 2008.

Sennett, Richard: *The Craftsman*, New Haven, Conn., Yale University Press, 2008.

Shaughnessy, Adrian: *How to Be a Graphic Designer without Losing your Soul*, New York, Princeton Architectural Press, 2005.

Shaughnessy, Adrian: *Look at This: Contemporary Brochures, Catalogues & Documents*, London, Laurence King Publishers, 2006.

Sherin, Aaris: *SustainAble: A Handbook of Materials and Applications for Graphic Designers and their Clients*, Beverly, Rockport Publishers, 2008.

Simonson, Alex; Schmitt, Bernd H.: *Marketing Aesthetics: The Strategic Management of Brands, Identity and Image*, New York, Free Press, 1997.

Snyder, Gertrude; Peckolick, Alan: *Herb Lubalin: Art Director, Graphic Designer and Typographer*, New York, American Showcase, 1988.

Stankowski, Jochen: *Signs*, bilingual edition, Köln, Walther König, 2005.

Visocky O'Grady, Jennifer; Visocky O'Grady, Kenneth: *The Information Design Handbook*, Cincinnati, How Books, 2008.

Yelavich, Susan: *Profile: Pentagram Design*, London, Phaidon, 2004.

Proudly presents

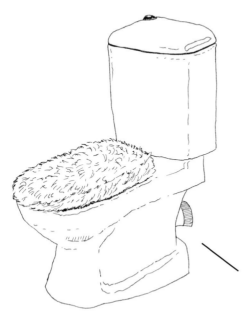

Ana Labudović
Freelance designer and editor
Barcelona, Spain/Zagreb, Croatia
The bumpy ride: at nineteen she began working as a graphic designer in an advertising agency, moved on to a Web-oriented studio, and organized music and video events on the side. She took off to Sweden to study digital media at Hyper Island and specialized in project management, moved to Barcelona for a design internship at Vasava Artworks, after which she decided to start freelancing. Her first book, *Color in Graphics,* was published in 2008.
www.ana-labudovic.com

Ana leaves the toilet seat down 74.8% of the time.

Nenad Vukušić
Freelance multidisciplinary thinker and writer
Zagreb, Croatia
At nineteen he ran away from home to study literature instead of becoming a dentist. Since then he has worked as a journalist, written copy for dozens of agencies, won some international advertizing awards, and moved on to scriptwriting and music video directing. This is his first book.
www.vukusic.org

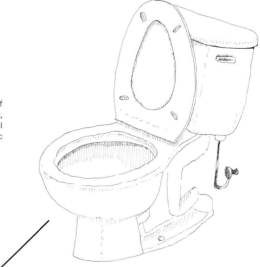

Nenad leaves the toilet seat down 25.2% of the time.

THANKS = 100%

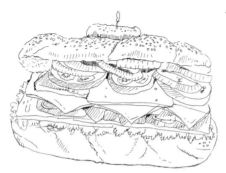

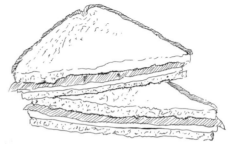

Thank you!

We'd like to thank all the studios, designers and nondesigners who participated in creating this book—we learned so much through interviewing them and found ourselves quite inspired.

A very special thanks goes out to our illustrator, José Manuel Hortelano Pi—the best illustrator we've never met! His contribution was priceless.

Another special thanks goes to our proofreader, text-Botoxer, and sometimes even extreme makeoverist, Cindy Blazevic, who had to put up with rough deadlines, weird ideas, and pigeon English.

Honorable mentions go to the following websites that kindly helped us conduct our survey:

swisslegacy.com
thestylepress.net
pingmag.jp
reformrevolution.com
graphicdesignbasics.com
effektiveblog.com
fuelyourcreativity.com

Finally, we'd like to thank both our biological and nonbiological families and friends, as well as each other.